Achieving Assessment Goals Using Evaluation Techniques

Peter J. Gray, *Editor*
Syracuse University

NEW DIRECTIONS FOR HIGHER EDUCATION
MARTIN KRAMER, *Editor-in-Chief*
University of California, Berkeley

Number 67, Fall 1989

Paperback sourcebooks in
The Jossey-Bass Higher Education Series

Jossey-Bass Inc., Publishers
San Francisco • Oxford

Peter J. Gray (ed.).
Achieving Assessment Goals Using Evaluation Techniques.
New Directions for Higher Education, no. 67.
Volume XVII, number 3.
San Francisco: Jossey-Bass, 1989.

New Directions for Higher Education
Martin Kramer, *Editor-in-Chief*

Copyright © 1989 by Jossey-Bass Inc., Publishers

Copyright under International, Pan American, and Universal Copyright Conventions. All rights reserved. No part of this issue may be reproduced in any form—except for brief quotation (not to exceed 500 words) in a review or professional work—without permission in writing from the publishers.

New Directions for Higher Education is published quarterly by Jossey-Bass Inc., Publishers (publication number USPS 990-880). *New Directions* is numbered sequentially—please order extra copies by sequential number. The volume and issue numbers above are included for the convenience of libraries. Second-class postage paid at San Francisco, California, and at additional mailing offices. POSTMASTER: Send address changes to Jossey-Bass Inc., Publishers, 350 Sansome Street, San Francisco, California 94104.

Editorial correspondence should be sent to the Editor-in-Chief, Martin Kramer, 2807 Shasta Road, Berkeley, California 94708.

Library of Congress Catalog Card Number LC 85-644752

International Standard Serial Number ISSN 0271-0560

International Standard Book Number ISBN 1-55542-846-0

Cover art by WILLI BAUM

Manufactured in the United States of America. Printed on acid-free paper.

Ordering Information

The paperback sourcebooks listed below are published quarterly and can be ordered either by subscription or single copy.

Subscriptions cost $56.00 per year for institutions, agencies, and libraries. Individuals can subscribe at the special rate of $42.00 per year *if payment is by personal check*. (Note that the full rate of $56.00 applies if payment is by institutional check, even if the subscription is designated for an individual.) Standing orders are accepted.

Single copies are available at $12.95 when payment accompanies order. (California, New Jersey, New York, and Washington, D.C., residents please include appropriate sales tax.) For billed orders, cost per copy is $12.95 plus postage and handling.

Substantial discounts are offered to organizations and individuals wishing to purchase bulk quantities of Jossey-Bass sourcebooks. Please inquire.

Please note that these prices are for the calendar year 1989 and are subject to change without notice. Also, some titles may be out of print and therefore not available for sale.

To ensure correct and prompt delivery, all orders must give either the *name of an individual* or an *official purchase order number*. Please submit your order as follows:

Subscriptions: specify series and year subscription is to begin.
Single Copies: specify sourcebook code (such as, HE1) and first two words of title.

Mail orders to:
Jossey-Bass Inc., Publishers
350 Sansome Street
San Francisco, California 94104

New Directions for Higher Education Series
Martin Kramer, *Editor-in-Chief*

HE1   *Facilitating Faculty Development,* Mervin Freedman
HE2   *Strategies for Budgeting,* George Kaludis
HE3   *Services for Students,* Joseph Katz

HE4	*Evaluating Learning and Teaching,* C. Robert Pace
HE5	*Encountering the Unionized University,* Jack H. Schuster
HE6	*Implementing Field Experience Education,* John Duley
HE7	*Avoiding Conflict in Faculty Personnel Practices,* Richard Peairs
HE8	*Improving Statewide Planning,* James L. Wattenbarger, Louis W. Bender
HE9	*Planning the Future of the Undergraduate College,* Donald G. Trites
HE10	*Individualizing Education by Learning Contracts,* Neal R. Berte
HE11	*Meeting Women's New Educational Needs,* Clare Rose
HE12	*Strategies for Significant Survival,* Clifford T. Stewart, Thomas R. Harvey
HE13	*Promoting Consumer Protection for Students,* Joan S. Stark
HE14	*Expanding Recurrent and Nonformal Education,* David Harman
HE15	*A Comprehensive Approach to Institutional Development,* William Bergquist, William Shoemaker
HE16	*Improving Educational Outcomes,* Oscar Lenning
HE17	*Renewing and Evaluating Teaching,* John A. Centra
HE18	*Redefining Service, Research, and Teaching,* Warren Bryan Martin
HE19	*Managing Turbulence and Change,* John D. Millett
HE20	*Increasing Basic Skills by Developmental Studies,* John E. Roueche
HE21	*Marketing Higher Education,* David W. Barton, Jr.
HE22	*Developing and Evaluating Administrative Leadership,* Charles F. Fisher
HE23	*Admitting and Assisting Students After Bakke,* Alexander W. Astin, Bruce Fuller, Kenneth C. Green
HE24	*Institutional Renewal Through the Improvement of Teaching,* Jerry G. Gaff
HE25	*Assuring Access for the Handicapped,* Martha Ross Redden
HE26	*Assessing Financial Health,* Carol Frances, Sharon L. Coldren
HE27	*Building Bridges to the Public,* Louis T. Benezet, Frances W. Magnusson
HE28	*Preparing for the New Decade,* Larry W. Jones, Franz A. Nowotny
HE29	*Educating Learners of All Ages,* Elinor Greenberg, Kathleen M. O'Donnell, William Bergquist
HE30	*Managing Facilities More Effectively,* Harvey H. Kaiser
HE31	*Rethinking College Responsibilities for Values,* Mary Louise McBee
HE32	*Resolving Conflict in Higher Education,* Jane E. McCarthy
HE33	*Professional Ethics in University Administration,* Ronald H. Stein, M. Carlota Baca
HE34	*New Approaches to Energy Conservation,* Sidney G. Tickton
HE35	*Management Science Applications to Academic Administration,* James A. Wilson
HE36	*Academic Leaders as Managers,* Robert H. Atwell, Madeleine F. Green
HE37	*Designing Academic Program Reviews,* Richard F. Wilson
HE38	*Successful Responses to Financial Difficulties,* Carol Frances
HE39	*Priorities for Academic Libraries,* Thomas J. Galvin, Beverly P. Lynch
HE40	*Meeting Student Aid Needs in a Period of Retrenchment,* Martin Kramer
HE41	*Issues in Faculty Personnel Policies,* Jon W. Fuller
HE42	*Management Techniques for Small and Specialized Institutions,* Andrew J. Falender, John C. Merson
HE43	*Meeting the New Demand for Standards,* Jonathan R. Warren
HE44	*The Expanding Role of Telecommunications in Higher Education,* Pamela J. Tate, Marilyn Kressel
HE45	*Women in Higher Education Administration,* Adrian Tinsley, Cynthia Secor, Sheila Kaplan

HE46 *Keeping Graduate Programs Responsive to National Needs,*
Michael J. Pelczar, Jr., Lewis C. Solomon
HE47 *Leadership Roles of Chief Academic Officers,* David G. Brown
HE48 *Financial Incentives for Academic Quality,* John Folger
HE49 *Leadership and Institutional Renewal,* Ralph M. Davis
HE50 *Applying Corporate Management Strategies,* Roger J. Flecher
HE51 *Incentive for Faculty Vitality,* Roger G. Baldwin
HE52 *Making the Budget Process Work,* David J. Berg, Gerald M. Skogley
HE53 *Managing College Enrollments,* Don Hossler
HE54 *Institutional Revival: Case Histories,* Douglas W. Steeples
HE55 *Crisis Management in Higher Education,* Hal Hoverland, Pat McInturff, C. E. Tapie Rohm, Jr.
HE56 *Managing Programs for Learning Outside the Classroom,*
Patricia Senn Breivik
HE57 *Creating Career Programs in a Liberal Arts Context,* Mary Ann F. Rehnke
HE58 *Financing Higher Education: Strategies After Tax Reform,*
Richard E. Anderson, Joel W. Meyerson
HE59 *Student Outcomes Assessment: What Institutions Stand to Gain,*
Diane F. Halpern
HE60 *Increasing Retention: Academic and Student Affairs Administrators in Partnership,* Martha McGinty Stodt, William M. Klepper
HE61 *Leaders on Leadership: The College Presidency,* James L. Fisher, Martha W. Tack
HE62 *Making Computers Work for Administrators,* Kenneth C. Green, Steven W. Gilbert
HE63 *Research Administration and Technology Transfer,* James T. Kenny
HE64 *Successful Strategic Planning: Case Studies,* Douglas W. Steeples
HE65 *The End of Mandatory Retirement: Effects on Higher Education,*
Karen C. Holden, W. Lee Hansen
HE66 *Improving Undergraduate Education in Large Universities,*
Carol H. Pazandak

Contents

Editor's Notes   1
Peter J. Gray

1. Demystifying Assessment: Learning from the Field of Evaluation   5
Barbara Gross Davis
Assessment practitioners can learn much from the knowledge and good practices achieved in the field of evaluation.

2. An Organizational Perspective for the Effective Practice of Assessment   21
G. Roger Sell
Critical organizational realities temper assessment practices.

3. So, What's the Use?   43
Larry A. Braskamp
Experience suggests five guidelines and their implications for assessment.

4. Assessment and Academic Judgments in Higher Education   51
George M. Dennison, Mary Anne Bunda
Assessment is a method to provide data that perhaps will be useful to evaluation.

5. A Role for Assessment in Higher Education Decision Making   71
John C. Ory
Assessment may serve various needs for information within the context of evaluation programs.

6. Improving Higher Education: The Need for a Broad View of Assessment   89
Peter J. Gray, Robert M. Diamond
A broad definition of assessment is useful in dealing with a number of issues in higher education.

7. Making Assessment Work: A Synthesis and Future Directions   109
G. Roger Sell
Advice synthesized from the preceding chapters can help readers determine the future of assessment in their own institutions.

Index   121

Editor's Notes

Student outcome assessment has been used in higher education since the introduction of "the senior declamation and oral examination—public ways of validating the learning of graduates—[which] were common in the nineteenth-century American college" (Marchese, 1987, p. 3). In recent years, however, such assessment has taken on new importance as a result of various national reports (National Institute of Education, 1984), books (Bok, 1986), articles (Hutchings, 1987), and conferences (such as the American Association for Higher Education's annual assessment forum).

Student outcome assessment for the purpose of student development and institutional accountability was the initial focus of the current assessment movement. But the scope of assessment has been expanded considerably to include a broad view of assessment purposes and processes. Now "serious assessment is nothing less than the institutionalization of self-awareness and constant change, that is, continuous self-renewal" (Spangehl, 1987, p. 35). And, as Peter Ewell (1987) points out, "shifting the focus . . . toward innovation and improvement . . . reinforces a challenge that has been with us since the emergence of assessment as a national issue: We need to find much better ways of using assessment information in institutional and curricular decision making" (p. 28).

These statements not only help to define the purpose of assessment in broad terms but they also emphasize a need to enhance the utilization of assessment information in a wide range of decisions. Such definitions of assessment have emerged because the narrow point of view—measuring student outcomes for the purpose of accountability—ignores the great variety of issues that are facing institutions of higher education, has major methodological limitations, and raises serious political concerns regarding control and organizational concerns regarding resources.

The leaders of the assessment movement have realized that they must embrace this broader view of assessment because it allows them to consider an appropriately diverse set of reasons for doing assessment; it provides the framework for conducting more comprehensive, thorough, and valid assessments; and it offers a structure for including a wide group of stakeholders. All of this serves to make assessment more credible and palatable to those being evaluated—namely, institutions and their faculty. In turn, this makes it more likely that quality assessment will, in fact, take place and that the results will be used.

However, a lack of focus on the reasons for assessment continues to exist on the part of individual institutions; "in their scramble to discover the *what* and *how* of assessment, institutions [may] forget *why* they are engaging in the process in the first place" (Ewell, 1987, p. 28). It may be that some institutions have not *forgotten* why but that they have never *known* why they were engaging in assessment (except for some need for external accountability). In addition, they may not have a history of conducting assessment studies and may lack the trained personnel and other institutional resources needed. Therefore, due to considerable external pressure and the lack of internal resources, their initial concern is understandably with what they should do and how they should do it.

In the past, evaluators and others have also realized that a broad view must be taken in order to best serve their clients. In response, they too have widened their scope, expanded their methodological repertoire, and diversified their stakeholder groups. The lessons learned by these other movements have much to teach those involved in the current assessment movement. By studying these lessons, some of the mistakes made in the past can be avoided, the assessment movement can mature more quickly, and those responsible for assessment can gain a clearer vision of what lies ahead.

Two alternative futures for assessment have emerged and are discussed in this volume. One is to broaden the definition of assessment to include a variety of activities that were formerly identified with evaluation, program review, accreditation, and so on. In effect, this option defines assessment as equivalent to these other processes. A second option retains the definition of assessment as the measurement of student outcomes but sees it as just one of many techniques for providing data within the context of a more comprehensive process like evaluation. Due to limitations of space, we were not able to include here a chapter by Lincoln (1988) that discusses a third option. This option calls for evaluation to play a mediating role among assessment, program review, and other processes currently vying for resources in higher education institutions.

The chapters in this sourcebook are intended to help all of those concerned with assessment in higher education to learn from the past and look toward the future. Over the last twenty years, the authors have provided assessment information, in a broad sense, on their campuses. They have done so within the context of the first two alternative futures just described. Together they have over a century of experience in designing and implementing studies and using their results to improve higher education.

In Chapter One, Davis discusses the extensive body of knowledge and good practice developed within the field of evaluation. An analysis of the current state of the assessment field and its relationship to the field of evaluation is presented using a framework of ten questions. Many specific examples are provided to illustrate the potential contribution of evaluation to the field of assessment.

In Chapter Two, Sell notes two of the most challenging aspects of assessment for administrators and faculty. The first is to balance needs for assessment with other institutional responsibilities. The second is to maintain a proper emphasis on assessment for accountability versus assessment for the continuing development and improvement of performance. Critics claim that higher education assessment is not occurring, but four types of assessment do routinely take place: student, faculty, program, and institutional. Sell looks at the critical organizational realities that temper these assessment practices and suggests ways to make assessment work within institutional constraints and expectations.

In Chapter Three, Braskamp reflects on his experience to help readers determine what the use is of doing assessment. He lays out five guidelines that should be considered in designing and implementing assessment studies and discusses their implications.

In Chapter Four, Dennison and Bunda differentiate between evaluation and assessment by characterizing assessment as a method or group of methods designed to accumulate information *perhaps* useful as evidence in an evaluation. They use a series of examples to describe assessment at their institution, and they offer a set of premises that will help to ensure good internal evaluation efforts because of the relevant and reliable information provided by assessment.

In Chapter Five, Ory describes a variety of evaluation programs to illustrate the needs for and uses made of assessment information. He addresses the issues of credibility, organizational fit, utility, and flexibility, and he discusses the campus needs that were met through these evaluation programs.

In Chapter Six, Gray and Diamond define assessment and evaluation as systematic data collection processes intended to provide information that will direct action. They describe a set of essential elements that may be used to conduct studies on courses, curricula, and academic or nonacademic programs; administrative concerns; and institutional issues. Examples from their own studies illustrate how a comprehensive process combined with a broad set of purposes can help to address the wide range of information needs that exist in higher education institutions.

In Chapter Seven, Sell summarizes the differences in opinion that have been presented by the authors. In addition, some advice is synthesized from the preceding chapters that will help readers guide the future direction of assessment in their own institutions.

Peter J. Gray
Editor

References

Bok, D. C. *Higher Learning.* Cambridge, Mass.: Harvard University Press, 1986.
Ewell, P. T. "Assessment: Where Are We?" *Change,* January/February 1987, pp. 23-28.

Hutchings, P. "Six Stories: Implementing Successful Assessment." *Journal of Staff, Program, and Organizational Development,* 1987, 5, 4.

Lincoln, Y. S. "Can Somebody Give Me a Hand Here? Program Review, Accreditation Processes, and Outcome Assessment as the Straws That Are Breaking the Camel's Back." Paper presented at the annual meeting of the Association for the Study of Higher Education, St. Louis, Mo., November 3, 1988.

Marchese, T. J. "An Update on Assessment." *AAHE Bulletin,* December 1987, pp. 3-8.

National Institute of Education, Study Group on the Conditions of Excellence in American Higher Education. *Involvement in Learning: Realizing the Potential of American Higher Education.* Washington, D.C.: U.S. Government Printing Office, 1984.

Spangehl, S. D. "The Push to Assess." *Change,* January/February 1987, pp. 35-39.

Peter J. Gray is director of evaluation and research at the Syracuse University Center for Instructional Development, and he is a member of the American Evaluation Association board of directors.

The challenge confronting those undertaking assessment efforts is to make use of the extensive body of knowledge and good practices developed within the field of evaluation.

Demystifying Assessment: Learning from the Field of Evaluation

Barbara Gross Davis

In the last four years since the assessment movement began, the following developments have occurred: (1) All but fourteen state legislatures have taken action to consider or begin campus assessment programs (National Governors' Association, 1988). Some forty states now require assessment by state law or policy (Blumenstyk, 1988). (2) Accreditation agencies are requesting assessments of student achievement as critical elements in the accrediting process. (3) The Fund for the Improvement of Postsecondary Education (FIPSE) has awarded assessment-related grants to over twenty institutions and organizations. (4) Three national conferences have been held on assessment, the most recent attracting over 1,000 people. (5) Special issues of professional journals have been devoted to assessment; in the last three years, four Jossey-Bass sourcebooks have appeared on this topic (Banta 1988; Bray and Belcher, 1987; Ewell, 1985; Halpern, 1987). (6) Offices of assessment have sprung up at colleges and universities across the country. (7) The testing industry has been aggressively developing new instruments to measure students' cognitive growth and personal development.

As others have pointed out (Ewell, 1988), there is nothing terribly new about higher education's attempt to assess itself. For decades, higher education has assessed student learning and demonstrated institutional effectiveness to external agencies. So, why the flurry of activity at this time?

Observers (Rossman and El-Khawas, 1987; Westling, 1988) have speculated on how economic, social, and political concerns have converged to create a welcome climate for assessment. First, the public perceives that college students often lack basic skills on entry and at graduation. New demands in the workplace for greater sophistication in writing, reading, and computing may have magnified college graduates' weaknesses. Second, the perceived failings of higher education, as documented by several books and national reports, have created a crisis of confidence and led to calls for improving the educational system. And education, critics argue, should be judged by assessment; traditional measures of student achievement, such as course grades and retention and graduation rates, do not satisfy these critics' standards for reliability and interpretability across programs and institutions.

Political pressures have also played a role. State legislators know that "creating better schools" is a popular campaign theme, and tight budgets lead public officials to demand accountability and proof of cost effectiveness. Assessment thus becomes the lever helping states to meet their economic and social goals: "It is essential that states maintain the pressure to assess despite the many vocal arguments against it" (National Governors' Association, 1988, p. 42).

In the rush to meet external demands for assessment, those involved in assessment have overlooked what the field of evaluation can contribute to their endeavors. To bring some order to the diverse literature of the assessment movement and to show more clearly the contributions evaluation can make to assessment, this chapter analyzes assessment using the conceptualization of educational evaluation put forth by Stufflebeam (1974) and expanded by Nevo (1986). Ten questions provide the framework for this analysis:

1. What does the term *assessment* mean?
2. What is the purpose of assessment?
3. What can be assessed?
4. What kinds of questions can be asked in assessment?
5. What criteria can be used to judge the merit or worth of what has been assessed?
6. Who should be served by assessment?
7. What are the procedures for conducting an assessment?
8. What methods of inquiry can be used in assessment?
9. Who should do an assessment?
10. By what standards is assessment judged?

What Does the Term *Assessment* Mean?

Despite increasing nationwide attention to the topic of assessment, there is no consensus on exactly what topics and processes assessment comprises. Is the primary concern to be assessment of the performance of individual students or groups of students, the effectiveness of instructional practices, or the functioning of departments or the institution itself? Various definitions are in widespread use.

Some writers (Boyer and Ewell, 1988; Bray and Belcher, 1987; Eison and Palladino, 1988) approach assessment broadly, describing it as encompassing general activities of testing, evaluation, and documentation. For example, Boyer and Ewell (1988) define assessment as "processes that provide information about individual students, about curricula or programs, about institutions, or about entire systems of institutions." Others equate *assessment* and *evaluation*, using the terms interchangeably.

Still others view assessment narrowly, as specifically tied to student learning, knowledge, skills, and outcomes (Marchese, 1987; Jacobi, Astin, and Ayala, 1987; National Governors' Association, 1988). For this group, assessment encompasses various procedures that determine the extent to which students have met curricular goals, mastered the prescribed subject matter, and acquired the skills and characteristics essential to an educated person (Chandler, 1986). Recognizing the confusion in terminology, some researchers speak about outcomes assessment (Banta, 1988) or assessment of student learning (Adelman, 1988) when referring to assessment and student performance. But many writers simply use the term *assessment* as shorthand notation for measuring student achievement and development.

The problems in defining assessment are similar to those encountered in defining evaluation in the early years of the development of the field. Many definitions of evaluation have been proposed and used (Nevo, 1986). For example, in the 1950s evaluation was defined as the process of determining the extent to which educational objectives are being met. (Note the similarity to Chandler's definition of assessment as the extent to which individual students meet curricular goals.) In the 1960s and early 1970s, evaluation was defined as the process of providing information for decision makers (Note the similarity to Boyer's and Ewell's definition of assessment as the process of providing information about students, curricula, programs, and institutions.) More recently, a broader definition has been adopted by evaluators: Evaluation is the process of determining the worth or merit of an activity, program, person, or product (Joint Committee, 1981). The special features of evaluation, as a particular kind of investigation, include concerns with needs, description, context, outcomes, comparisons, costs, audience, utilization, and the supporting and making of sound value judgments.

It may be that the field of assessment will evolve in much the same manner. But the assessment movement seems to be making little use of what is known about evaluation. For example, a glossary of assessment terminology (Boyer and Ewell, 1988) does not include an entry for "evaluation," and few writers in assessment make referencce to the body of evaluation theory and practice.

Given the lack of consensus on what constitutes assessment, we cannot be surprised that there is little agreement on the relationship between the terms *assessment* and *evaluation*. Prior to the growth of the assessment movement, those in the evaluation field sometimes used assessment as a synonym for evaluation. Even then, however, there was a sense that the two were not completely interchangeable. As Scriven (1981) points out, assessment tends to focus more on quantitative or testing approaches, as exemplified by the National Assessment of Educational Progress.

Today, one finds three stances: that evaluation is a subset of assessment, that assessment is a subset of evaluation, that evaluation and assessment are converging. The first is proffered by some in the assessment movement who consider evaluation to be the program or curricular evaluation component of assessment. But this is an inaccurate view, since evaluation encompasses more than programs and curricula.

The second view relies on a narrow definition of assessment focusing on student achievement and development. In fact, "outcome evaluation," or "impact assessment," is an accepted component of evaluation (Rossi and Freeman, 1985; Posavac and Carey, 1985), investigating the results, impact, or outcomes of a program or intervention.

If a broad definition of assessment is adopted, then assessment and evaluation begin to merge into a common effort to understand and judge the merit and worth of teaching and learning within a course, curriculum, educational program, sequence of study, department, unit, or institution.

What Is the Purpose of Assessment?

In the assessment literature, one tends to find statements of wide-ranging purposes. For example, Ewell (1988) cites the following: to evaluate curricula, to demonstrate external accountability, to recruit students, to raise funds for institutions, and to change the way teaching and learning occur in individual classrooms. Jacobi, Astin, and Ayala (1987) identify these purposes of assessment: to provide information about students' change and development, to establish accountability for external agencies, to evaluate programs, to analyze cost-effectiveness, and to set goals.

From the field of evaluation comes a more meaningful, less complex, conceptually clearer way to think about the purposes of assessment. A major distinction is made between formative and summative evaluation. Formative evaluation is undertaken for the purpose of improving and developing an activity, program, person, or product. Summative evaluation is undertaken for the purposes of accountability or resource allocation (in the case of programs), for certification, selection, and placement (in the case of students), or for decisions about merit increases and promotions (in the case of faculty). Similarly, we can say that institutions undertake assessments to improve what they are doing (formative) or to make decisions about resources, institutions, programs, faculty, or students (summative). Some writers (Ewell and Boyer, 1988) have grasped the importance of the distinction, but others have overlooked it and therefore have also ignored how the purpose of an assessment influences aspects of its design and analysis.

By borrowing concepts from evaluation, we have highlighted key differences between formative and summative assessment in Figure 1.

What Can Be Assessed?

Those who adopt a broad view of assessment see all aspects of higher education as subjects for assessment: students, educational and administrative personnel, curricula, programs, departments, and institutions.

Figure 1. Formative Versus Summative Assessment

Feature	Formative Assessment	Summative Assessment
Purpose	Improvement or development of activities, programs, products, people	Accountability, resource allocation; selection, placement, certification; pay and promotion decisions
Audience	Internal decision maker: program or department administrators; individual faculty	External decision maker: central administrators; government officials; accrediting bodies; public
Scope	Diagnostic, detailed, specific assessments	Global assessments
Procedures	Informal; narrow; specialized	Formal; comprehensive
Timing	Ongoing or during a program or sequence of study	Before and after or simply at the completion of a program or sequence of study
Sources of Information	One or more	Multiple and diverse
Emphasis	Suggestions for improvement	Overall judgments

Under this broad definition, assessment includes the many program reviews, self-studies, faculty evaluations, special-project evaluations, and so on that institutions routinely conduct to gather data about their effectiveness. Here are examples of such regularly scheduled activities at the University of California at Berkeley:

- Peer reviews (including student and faculty surveys as well as interview data) of all undergraduate and graduate programs conducted on a regular review cycle
- Peer reviews of the quality of teaching of every faculty member as part of the regular merit and promotion process
- Annual surveys of entering freshmen regarding students' backgrounds, interests, aspirations, and attitudes
- Placement tests in mathematics and composition used to determine students' skill levels
- Surveys of students in every class each semester about the effectiveness of the course and the teaching performance of the instructor
- Department, college, and campuswide surveys conducted periodically of graduating seniors and alumni regarding their opinion of the education they have received
- Occasional surveys of employers of graduates conducted by individual departments
- Exit interviews with students who leave the campus before graduation
- Review of ethnic diversity of applicants, enrollees, graduates, and dropouts
- Review and analysis of retention rates for students in aggregate and by various subgroups
- Formative and summative evaluation of individual support units and student services, such as the counseling center.

One would think that such information would interest public and state legislatures concerned about assessment. But these data are often overlooked, and special assessment reports are sought instead. The institutions are partly to blame in that they sometimes provide so much data in such detail, without a framework for interpreting their significance, that legislators dismiss the information as just another numbing report. There is also the problem with self-reports: If an institution prepares a negative report, its credibility is usually not questioned. But, for many external audiences, positive self-reports are highly suspect or simply not believed. The final blow against data from routine reviews and surveys is precisely that they are routine. Legislators and the public want to know what is new. The same high levels of accomplishment, reported year after year, may not satisfy external audiences. This demand for news challenges institutions that have been regularly reporting routine data to recast the information and present it as special assessment data.

Those who adopt a narrow view of assessment focus on the student outcomes of higher education. Even with such a view, there are still many possible outcomes. Virtually every human characteristic can be assessed (Baird, 1988a): knowledge, skills, attitudes, values, and behaviors. The problem, then, is not deciding what to assess but deciding how to select the outcomes to be examined. These choices depend on the values and priorities of those commissioning the assessment and those who will actually or potentially use the results (called "stakeholders" in evaluation terminology), as well as on the practical constraints of time, resources, and tools to measure outcomes.

What Kinds of Questions Can Be Asked in Assessment?

The best place to begin any investigation is to define the questions of most interest to the stakeholders—the potential users and audience. In evaluation, emphasis is placed on identifying and asking questions of most interest to decision makers, program participants, and the audiences for the evaluation. A wide range of questions are generated, refined, and narrowed down to those that can be answered given the resource constraints, the interests of the stakeholders, and the circumstances for the evaluation.

This same approach can be used to generate assessment questions. Here are some examples of questions generated, in part, by faculty members of the University of California at a conference called "Assessing the Lower Division," held at the University of California at Los Angeles, in February 1989:

1. *Who applies to and enrolls in the university, and how well prepared are these students?* For summative assessment, information about applicants and new students is a measure of an institution's quality—whether it can recruit and enroll high-ability students—and also a measure of how well the institution is enrolling underrepresented minority students. For formative assessment, information about new enrollments is critical in giving faculty an understanding of the abilities and preparation of the students they will be teaching. Measures that help answer this question include demographic characteristics of students, students' standardized test scores and high school performance, percentage of students in the upper 5 percent or 10 percent of their graduating class who apply and enroll in the university, number of valedictorians and number of National Merit Scholars, and pass rates on campus freshman placement exams in composition and mathematics.

2. *What do students learn?* The specific aspects of learning to be investigated will depend on the values and priorities of individual institutions. Here are some components of student learning, with an indication of data sources for answering the question:

- *What type of education is represented by the courses students take?* Do the courses students take exemplify the university's concept of a good education? Source: analysis of students' transcripts to identify course-taking patterns.
- *Does the undergraduate experience develop qualities valued in educated persons?* Such qualities might include critical thinking, problem solving, mastery of general skills, and an understanding of the contemporary world. Sources: transcript analysis; review of course syllabuses; senior theses or projects; comprehensive exams, if available; survey of faculty and students.
- *Have students developed aesthetic interests and an appreciation of the arts?* Sources: transcript analysis; student attendance at campus museums and performing arts events; number of submissions to campus arts award programs; use of campus arts facilities such as darkrooms and pottery studios; student participation in arts clubs.
- *To what extent can students communicate in writing with clarity and style?* Sources: transcript analysis; junior-level writing exams, if offered; portfolios or collections of students' written work; student journals.
- *What is the course withdrawal rate?* Measures: percentage of total course registrations that resulted in withdrawals; percentage of individual students with at least one withdrawal.
- *How knowledgeable are graduating seniors?* Sources: Graduate Record Examination (GRE), Law School Admission Test (LSAT), and Medical College Admission Test (MCAT) test scores; senior theses, projects, comprehensive exams; external awards and recognition of students.

3. *What do students value?* Again, the priorities and values of each college and university will determine what is measured within this area. Here are some examples:

- *To what extent do students show interest in and respect for different cultures and different points of view?* Measures: analysis of racial, ethnic, and religious incidents that indicate bias, prejudice, or stereotyping; enrollments in courses dealing with ethnic, gender, and cultural diversity; number of applicants and enrollments in study-abroad programs.
- *To what extent are students socially responsible and involved in the community?* Measures: student participation in volunteer groups, charitable work, and the like; transcript analysis of field study courses and internships.

4. *Who is dropping out?* Through exit interviews or surveys, one can identify the reasons students withdraw: transfer to another institution, involuntary withdrawal (health or financial reasons), voluntary with-

drawal (job, marriage), or academic dismissal. Rates of attrition and retention can be calculated by major, gender, ethnicity, grade point average, and transfer status.

5. *What is the quality of undergraduate teaching?*
   - *Who teaches undergraduate courses, particularly in the lower division?* Measures: percentage of faculty who teach at least one undergraduate course per term; percentage of lower-division courses taught by faculty at each rank; percentage of undergraduate students by year in school who have had at least three regular faculty members during each term; differences among departments in allocating faculty to the lower division.
   - *How effective is undergraduate teaching?* Sources: student ratings by size of course, discipline, instructional method; alumni surveys; peer judgments of deans and faculty committees reviewing personnel cases.
   - *To what extent are faculty interested in undergraduate teaching?* Sources: course assignments by faculty teaching load and rank; faculty survey; faculty participation in instructional improvement activities.
   - *To what extent do lower-division students have opportunities for quality contact with professors?* Sources: student and faculty surveys; transcript analysis; use of office hours; number of faculty involved in advising.
   - *What is the level, nature, and quality of attention given by departments to the training of teaching assistants (TAs)?* Sources: percentages of departments that offer training for TAs; surveys of faculty and TAs.
   - *How effective are services provided to faculty and TAs for teaching improvement?* Source: evaluation of support services.

6. *What is the quality of the curriculum?*
   - *What reform efforts have taken place or are under way?* Sources: task force reports; changes in policy; comparison of catalogues before and after curriculum revision.
   - *How accessible are lower-division courses? Can students get into the courses that they need or want?* Sources: demands for enrollment; transcript analysis; student surveys.
   - *What is the effectiveness of the lower-division curriculum in satisfying students' needs to explore a diversity of subjects and to pursue a major?* Sources: materials available describing different majors; premajor advising programs; course-taking patterns through transcript analysis; length of drift before declaring a major; number of students who change majors; student performance in upper-division courses; student surveys.
   - *What is the quality of departments with large undergraduate enroll-*

ments? Sources: academic program reviews; alumni surveys; surveys of faculty and current students.
- *What are the class-size experiences of students?* Measures: percentage of lower-division students who have had at least one course each term that enrolled fifty or fewer students; percentage of lower-division students who have had all courses in their first year enrollment 100 or fewer students; percentage of lower-division students who have had at least one seminar class.

7. *How effective is the advising that students receive?* Who advises students about academic issues (selecting courses and programs of study), career options (career choices and opportunities for further education and training), and personal development (participation in extracurricular activities or job experiences)? Sources: student and alumni surveys on advisers' knowledge, availability, and rapport.

8. *How do students feel about their undergraduate experiences?* Sources: surveys of juniors or seniors; counseling reports on student problems; and ombudsman reports of students' experiences and complaints.

9. *How effective are support services?* Sources: surveys of students and faculty who use particular services.

10. *What happens to students after they graduate?* Sources: alumni surveys; graduate school admissions; job placements; follow-up surveys of employers of graduates.

What Criteria Can Be Used to Judge the Merit or Worth of What Has Been Assessed?

The assessment literature is largely silent on judging worth or merit. In contrast, in evaluation a variety of criteria has been offered for judging merit, and the evaluation literature stresses the importance of using multiple criteria for judging any program, activity, service, person, or object. Criteria may include the extent to which the entity being evaluated responds to identified needs of actual and potential clients; achieves national goals, ideals, or social values; meets agreed on standards and norms; outdoes or outperforms alternative objects; or achieves important stated goals (Nevo, 1986).

Judging merit does surface in discussions of value-added or talent-development assessment, which attempts, through pre- and posttesting, to estimate the portion of students' growth or development that can be reasonably attributed to specific educational experiences (the value added by participation in higher education). The assessment asks how a college education has changed students' knowledge, skills, and values, and those institutions that report greater changes are considered more successful. As Ewell (1988) points out, however, students may change greatly but still fall below acceptable standards: Are institutions to be judged primarily in terms of the amount of change or the levels students finally attain? Too, the pre- and posttest model betrays a reductive premise, that education is "addictive" rather than synergistic, multifaceted, and multicausal.

At heart, value-added and talent-development assessments are new terminology for an old fundamental issue in educational research: What are the net effects of an educational experience on students' cognitive and noncognitive development? This question has also been phrased more complexly as "What kinds of students change in what ways when exposed to what kinds of educational experiences?" (Pascarella, 1986). Yet, as the literature shows (Halpern, 1987; Pascarella, 1986; Warren, 1984; McMillan, 1988; Hanson, 1988; Baird, 1988b), reliable, meaningful value-added assessment is difficult to implement. The technical problems include the difficulties (such as regression effects, maturation effects, cohort incomparability, and so on) of measuring change and of unbundling the influence of education from other influences on student growth; the absence of reliable, valid, standardized instruments to measure meaningful educational outcomes beyond content knowledge; and the challenge of developing instruments sensitive enough to measure subtle changes in noncognitive areas.

Finally, even if we had the measures, there are the difficulties of attributing changes to the institution, its students' aptitude or prior achievements, or the quality of students' learning efforts. Research indicates that the largest effects on student growth and change are due to maturation, followed by, in order, effects due to attendance at any college, effects due to attendance at a particular college, and specific college experiences (Baird, 1988b).

Given these conceptual and technical problems, those in the assessment movement may wish to adapt the criteria used in evaluation to judge merit and worth (Nevo, 1986): fills a critical need; achieves universally recognized goals, ideals, or values; meets agreed-on standards and norms; outperforms competitors; achieves important stated goals.

Who Should Be Served by Assessment?

Many in the field of evaluation have adopted Guba and Lincoln's (1981) term *stakeholders* to refer to all the groups of persons having some actual or potential stake in the performance of the entity being evaluated. Stakeholders for an assessment might include the decision makers commissioning the investigation, policy makers with some interest in the results, state and federal officials, campus administrators, program participants, faculty, students, parents, taxpayers, and the public at large.

Baird (1988a) lists examples of the kinds of assessment questions different audiences might pose about a college or university:

1. *Parents:* How likely is my child to be admitted? What is the curric-

ulum like? What programs or facilities are available to meet my child's interests? What are the chances a student will drop out, get A's, or go on to graduate school? What is the daily experience of this college like? Is there a sense of community and a strong intellectual climate?

2. *Taxpayers:* What are the costs to the taxpayers of this institution? Is this college meeting the current and future needs of the state in the training it is providing students? Are there provisions for excellence and equity? Can students from families with limited means attend and graduate from this college? Does this college make a difference to the economy and culture of the state?

3. *Faculty:* What are the implications for the curriculum and for students of a rise in student careerism and a concern for wealth? What conditions promote research among the faculty? How good is the teaching?

Baird's examples reinforce three important points stressed in the evaluation literature (Nevo, 1986) that are directly applicable to assessment: (1) An investigation can have more than one client, audience, or stakeholder; (2) different audiences may have different information needs; (3) since the questions important to different audiences will affect the kind of information collected, the level of data analysis, and the form of reporting the results, the specific audiences and their specific needs must be identified at the early stages of planning the study.

What Are the Procedures for Conducting an Assessment?

Case studies of how to conduct an assessment are widely reported in the literature (Bray and Belcher, 1987; Banta, 1988; Ewell, 1985; Halpern, 1987). Typical advice includes: start small, develop incrementally, use existing data when possible, use multiple measures rather than single test scores, stress formative aspects, ensure support of top leadership, involve faculty during all phases of development and implementation, recognize and incorporate the institution's unique mission and history. In addition, descriptions of activities at the University of Tennessee, Alverno College, and Northeast Missouri State University are available (Halpern, 1987). But the assessment movement as a whole lacks a specific methodology, models, or theoretical perspectives to inform practice.

In contrast, over the last four decades the field of evaluation has evolved detailed methodologies and various models that describe processes for conducting evaluations. Though the specific steps in an evaluation may depend on the evaluator's theoretical bent, evaluators agree on the following general steps:

1. Focus the evaluation problem by defining the charge from the client and the constraints.

2. Identify various stakeholders and audiences.
3. Generate questions of interest to stakeholders.
4. Refine and limit questions through negotiation with vested parties so the questions can be addressed.
5. Determine the methodology: Specify for each question the instrument or data source (new or existing), the sample from whom data have been or need to be collected, the time frame for data collection (if gathering new data), the methods of analysis, and the intended use of the results.
6. Communicate the findings to stakeholders in ways that they can use the results.

What Methods of Inquiry Can Be Used in Assessment?

Both the evaluation field and the assessment movement make use of traditional educational research methods: tests, surveys, interviews, and observations using experimental and quasi-experimental designs. The assessment movement has concentrated primarily on these methods. In contrast, the evaluation field has developed and popularized a range of naturalistic methods and qualitative approaches (Guba and Lincoln, 1981; Lincoln and Guba, 1986; Patton, 1987) and has explored unusual methods of inquiry: jury trials, art criticism applied to educational evaluation, and modus operandi (Smith, 1981a, 1981b).

As Hutchings (1988) notes, there is a growing interest in assessment methods that give more qualitative and complete pictures of what students learn under what conditions. Here, the vitality in evaluation methodology can provide useful models.

Who Should Do an Assessment?

The assessment literature (Ewell, 1988; Mentkowski, 1988; Miller, 1988) stresses the importance of faculty involvement in each step of the assessment process. Researchers also recommend that assessment activities elicit the support and advocacy of influential opinion makers on campus. For conducting an assessment, Ewell recommends that a small separate office of assessment be set up, reporting to high-level policy makers.

Appelbaum (1988) advocates a team approach to assessment. The team must be collectively knowledgeable about relevant instructional goals, current directions in the area under study, and basic evaluation principles and practices. From the evaluation literature, one might add that the team should also include collective expertise in administration to plan and manage the effort, as well as strong interpersonal and communication skills (Davis, 1986).

By What Standards Is Assessment Judged?

The literature on evaluation utilization and evaluation standards has direct implications for assessment, but the findings have not been widely applied. For example, evaluators have developed a set of thirty standards for judging an evaluation (Joint Committee, 1981). These standards are divided into four major categories: utility (does the evaluation serve practical information needs?), feasibility (is the evaluation realistic and prudent?), propriety (does the evaluation conform to legal and ethical standards?), and accuracy (is the evaluation technically adequate?).

Regarding the utilization of evaluation, the literature (Alkin, Daillak, and White, 1979; Braskamp and Brown, 1980; Patton, 1985) identifies general conditions that promote the use of evaluation results. These include involving potential audiences in the process from the beginning; providing opportunities for ongoing discussion of findings between client and evaluator; garnering support of key administrators; ensuring that the data are valid, reliable, and credible; offering explicit recommendations; preparing brief reports that address the client's concerns; releasing results in a timely manner; and identifying one or more concerned individuals who will provide the leadership to ensure that the findings are acted on.

Conclusion

As this review has shown, evaluation has much to offer assessment. The challenge confronting those in assessment is to become familiar with and make use of the extensive body of knowledge and good practices developed within the field of evaluation. For example, from work in evaluation utilization, those facing assessment can learn how to gather information that is likely to be used, and evaluation methodology can provide models for expanding the repertoire of assessment methods in order to gain richer insights and greater understanding of the workings of higher education.

In addition, by reference to evaluation, the assessment movement may be able to defuse some of its critics who tend to view assessment as focusing solely on student outcomes. By linking evaluation and assessment, the two may merge into a common broad-based effort to understand and judge the merit and worth of higher education.

References

Adelman, C. (ed.). *Performance and Judgment.* Washington, D.C.: Superintendent of Documents, U.S. Government Printing Office, 1988.

Alkin, M. C., Daillak, R., and White, P. *Using Evaluations: Does Evaluation Make a Difference?* Newbury Park, Calif.: Sage, 1979.

Appelbaum, M. I. "Assessment Through the Major." In C. Adelman (ed.), *Performance and Judgment.* Washington, D.C.: Superintendent of Documents, U.S. Government Printing Office, 1988.

Baird, L. L. "A Map of Postsecondary Assessment." *Research in Higher Education,* 1988a, *28* (2), 99–115.

Baird, L. L. "Value-Added: Using Student Gains as Yardsticks of Learning." In C. Adelman (ed.), *Performance and Judgment.* Washington, D.C.: Superintendent of Documents, U.S. Government Printing Office, 1988b.

Banta, T. W. (ed.). *Implementing Outcomes Assessment: Promise and Perils.* New Directions for Institutional Research, no. 59. San Francisco: Jossey-Bass, 1988.

Blumenstyk, G. "Diversity Is Keynote of States' Efforts to Assess Students' Learning." *Chronicle of Higher Education,* July 20, 1988, pp. A17, A25–A26.

Boyer, C. M., and Ewell, P. T. *State-Based Approaches to Assessment in Undergraduate Education: A Glossary and Selected References.* Denver, Colo.: Education Commission of the States, 1988.

Braskamp, L. A., and Brown, R. D. (eds.). *Utilization of Evaluative Information.* New Directions for Program Evaluation, no. 5. San Francisco: Jossey-Bass, 1980.

Bray, D., and Belcher, M. J. (eds.). *Issues in Student Assessment.* New Directions for Community Colleges, no. 59. San Francisco: Jossey-Bass, 1987.

Chandler, J. W. "The Why, What, and Who of Assessment: The College Perspective." In Educational Testing Service, *Assessing the Outcomes of Higher Education.* Princeton, N.J.: Educational Testing Service, 1986.

Davis, B. G. (ed.). *Teaching of Evaluation Across the Disciplines.* New Directions in Program Evaluation, no. 29. San Francisco: Jossey-Bass, 1986.

Eison, J., and Palladino, J. "Psychology's Role in Assessment." *APA Monitor,* September 1988, p. 31.

Ewell, P. T. (ed.). *Assessing Educational Outcomes.* New Directions for Institutional Research, no. 47. San Francisco: Jossey-Bass, 1985.

Ewell, P. T. "Implementing Assessment: Some Organizational Issues." In T. W. Banta (ed.), *Implementing Outcomes Assessment: Promise and Perils.* New Directions for Institutional Research, no. 59. San Francisco: Jossey-Bass, 1988.

Ewell, P. T., and Boyer, C. M. "Acting Out State-Mandated Assessment." *Change,* July/August 1988, pp. 40–47.

Guba, E. G., and Lincoln, Y. S. *Effective Evaluation: Improving the Usefulness of Evaluation Results Through Responsive and Naturalistic Approaches.* San Francisco: Jossey-Bass, 1981.

Halpern, D. F. (ed.). *Student Outcomes Assessment: What Institutions Stand to Gain.* New Directions for Higher Education, no. 59. San Francisco: Jossey-Bass, 1987.

Hanson, G. R. "Critical Issues in the Assessment of Value Added in Education." In T. W. Banta (ed.), *Implementing Outcomes Assessment: Promise and Perils.* New Directions for Institutional Research, no. 59. San Francisco: Jossey-Bass, 1988.

Hutchings, P. "Report on Third National Conference on Assessment in Higher Education." *AAHE Bulletin,* October 1988, pp. 3–5.

Jacobi, M., Astin, A., and Ayala, F. *College Student Outcomes Assessment: A Talent Development Perspective.* ASHE-ERIC Higher Education Report, no. 7. Washington, D.C.: Association for the Study of Higher Education, 1987.

Joint Committee on Standards for Educational Evaluation. *Standards for Evaluations of Educational Programs, Projects, and Materials.* New York: McGraw-Hill, 1981.

Lincoln, Y. S., and Guba, E. G. *Naturalistic Inquiry.* Newbury Park, Calif.: Sage, 1985.
McMillan, J. H. "Beyond Value-Added Education." *Journal of Higher Education,* 1988, *59* (5), 564–579.
Marchese, T. J. "Third Down, Ten Years to Go." *AAHE Bulletin,* December 1987, pp. 3–8.
Mentkowski, M. "Faculty and Student Involvement in Institutional Assessment." Paper presented at the American Evaluation Association meeting, New Orleans, October 1988.
Miller, R. I. "Using Change Strategies to Implement Assessment Programs." In T. W. Banta (ed.), *Implementing Outcomes Assessment: Promise and Perils.* New Directions for Institutional Research, no. 59. San Francisco: Jossey-Bass, 1988.
National Governors' Association. *Results in Education: 1988.* Washington, D.C.: National Governors' Association, 1988.
Nevo, D. "The Conceptualization of Educational Evaluation: An Analytic Review of the Literature." In E. R. House (ed.), *New Directions in Educational Evaluation.* Philadelphia: Falmer Press, Taylor and Francis, 1986.
Pascarella, E. T. "Are Value-Added Analyses Valuable?" In Educational Testing Service, *Assessing the Outcomes of Higher Education.* Princeton, N.J.: Educational Testing Service, 1986.
Patton, M. Q. *Utilization-Focused Evaluation.* (2nd ed.) Newbury Park, Calif.: Sage, 1986.
Patton, M. Q. *Creative Evaluation.* (2nd ed.) Newbury Park, Calif.: Sage, 1987.
Posavac, E. J., and Carey, R. G. *Program Evaluation Methods and Case Studies.* (2nd ed.) Englewood Cliffs, N.J.: Prentice-Hall, 1985.
Rossi, P. H., and Freeman, H. E. *Evaluation: A Systematic Approach.* (3rd ed.) Newbury Park, Calif.: Sage, 1985.
Rossman, J. E., and El-Khawas, E. *Thinking About Assessment.* Washington, D.C.: American Council on Education and the American Association for Higher Education, 1987.
Scriven, M. *Evaluation Thesaurus.* Pt. Reyes, Calif.: Edgepress, 1981.
Smith, N. L. (ed.). *Metaphors for Evaluation.* Newbury Park, Calif.: Sage, 1981a.
Smith, N. L. (ed.). *New Techniques for Evaluation.* Newbury Park, Calif.: Sage, 1981b.
Stufflebeam, D. L. "Metaevaluation." Occasional paper, no. 3. Kalamazoo: Evaluation Center, Western Michigan University, 1974.
Warren, J. "The Blind Alley of Value-Added." *AAHE Bulletin,* September 1984, pp. 10–13.
Westling, J. "The Assessment Movement Is Based on a Misdiagnosis of the Malaise Afflicting American Higher Education." *Chronicle of Higher Education,* October 19, 1988, pp. B1–B2.

Barbara Gross Davis is director of the Office of Educational Development at the University of California, Berkeley.

A challenging aspect of assessment for administrators and faculty is to maintain a proper emphasis on assessment used for accountability versus assessment used for the continuing development and improvement of performance.

An Organizational Perspective for the Effective Practice of Assessment

G. Roger Sell

Although the current emphasis on assessment in higher education is the appraisal of student outcomes (Adelman, 1986, Ewell, 1985), colleges and universities engage in a wide variety of assessment activities. These activities focus not only on students but also on faculty, programs, and the institutions themselves. The treatment of assessment in this chapter reflects an organizational perspective that includes, but goes beyond, student assessment.

There is not a single organizational approach to the study of higher education institutions as organizations but rather several theoretical frameworks, such as bureaucratic (Blau, 1973), collegial (Millett, 1962, 1978), political (Baldridge, 1971), and organized anarchy (Cohen and March, 1974). While each of these approaches emphasizes particular features of and assumptions about colleges and universities, the essence of an organizational perspective is that it brings attention to collective concerns. These concerns include but are not limited to the acquisition of resources to maintain and develop the institution, the allocation of authority and the structure of decision-making processes, the design and performance of work, and the outcomes and impacts associated with an institution.

An organizational perspective on assessment can have a number of benefits. It can help reveal relationships among assessment activities and the use of scarce resources for them. It can help locate and diagnose competing purposes that assessment serves. It can help identify constraints as well as opportunities for assessment in the service of institutions. And it can help formulate actions to remove barriers and provide support for effective assessment practices.

This chapter begins with a broad description and critique of assessment activities in colleges and universities. The ideals of assessment are then discussed along with organizational realities that temper and restrain them. The chapter concludes with some suggested strategies for practicing assessment in such a way that its perils are reduced and its contributions are enhanced.

The Scope of Assessment in Higher Education Institutions

With the primary attention of assessment activities in higher education now focused on student outcomes, those who are calling for more and better assessment have emphasized approaches such as:

- Standardized tests of student knowledge, general as well as specialized
- Follow-up studies of graduates and their careers
- Student attrition and retention studies
- Surveys and interviews of students to discuss their perceptions of the quality of their educational experiences, the climate of their institutions, and gains from their educational experiences.

One might conclude from listening to and reading the claims of critics that colleges and universities are neglecting their assessment responsibilities—that little is done in the way of assessment in higher education. From an organizational perspective, however, higher education institutions have been and continue to be actively involved in a wide range of assessment activities. Often these activities are overlooked when assessment is limited to the appraisal of student outcomes using specific measures or techniques.

Most colleges and universities are already doing extensive work in assessment if we define the term *assessment* as a process for informing decisions and judgments through (1) framing questions; (2) designing or selecting instruments and procedures for collecting data; (3) collecting, analyzing, and interpreting data; and (4) reporting and using information that is derived from qualitative as well as quantitative data. Some might object to this broad definition (Hartle, 1986). However, in conversations as well as in the literature, the term *assessment* is often used interchangeably with terms such as *testing, evaluation,* and *appraisal*. While clarity and precision in the use of terminology is surely desirable, the purpose here is not to settle long-standing arguments about the proper domains of research, evaluation, assessment, and related concepts (for a discussion of these terms, see Schalock and Sell, 1971). Readers who are more comfortable with substituting *evaluation* or *appraisal* for the term *assessment* should do so.

The various assessment activities of higher education institutions can be grouped generally into four broad categories. These include student assessment, faculty assessment, program assessment, and institutional assessment.

Student Assessment. While the recent attention given to assessment has focused on measuring institutionwide student outcomes, the most frequent and often overlooked form of student assessment occurs in courses and academic departments (McMillan, 1988). Student assessment at the course and department levels frequently serves the primary purpose of awarding grades and credits. However, institutions also conduct student testing for selection and placement before students enroll in courses and sometimes after they matriculate. In addition, some colleges and departments use senior exams, internships, and major projects as capstone experiences for assessing student performance.

Faculty Assessment. Most institutions have at least annual reviews of faculty performance, some for merit salary increases, and virtually all institutions have periodic reviews of faculty for tenure and promotion decisions (Centra, 1979). Some institutions have implemented assessment procedures for the posttenure evaluation of faculty (Bennett and Chater, 1984; Licata, 1986). Faculty are also nominated and judged for distinguished teaching, research, and/or service awards (Beidler, 1986). Each of these activities is an example of some form of assessment as that concept is developed here.

Program Assessment. In addition to accreditation reviews of academic programs, many institutions have established procedures for internal reviews and self-studies of academic programs (Arns and Poland, 1980; Conrad and Wilson, 1985). Some institutional procedures and responses are linked to state-level program reviews (Barak, 1982; Ohio Board of Regents, 1979). Academic programs are also at times rated or ranked by external reviewers and peers at other institutions (Lawrence and Green, 1980).

Institutional Assessment. Each of the regional accrediting associations conducts periodic reviews of higher education institutions in their area. Self-studies and external visitors are usually part of these reviews. In addition, institutions respond to federal and/or state compliance reviews for affirmative action, auditing and data reporting, health and safety, and so forth. Colleges and universities have also initiated assessments associated with strategic planning and the annual budgeting process (Barak, 1986; Micek, 1980; Shirley and Volkwein, 1978).

A Critique of Assessment Practices

The claim of critics that most colleges and universities are ignoring or neglecting their assessment activities is simply off target. It is not that institutions fail to engage in assessment; rather, institutions may lack systematic and reflective examinations of the purposes that assessment serves and the compatibility of practices with realizing the selected purposes. It would appear that the large portion of assessment activities in universities and colleges is directed more at summary descriptions and periodic judgments about quality than at specific diagnoses for the improvement of performance. Examples of this counterclaim are provided for each of the major groupings of assessment activities.

Student Assessment. Even when we change our instructional objectives, materials, or procedures, it is not uncommon that we use the same tests or other performance measures of student achievement. Student assessment can be conducted on the basis of expediency, habit, or external pressure rather than for ensuring that what we try to assess is worthy of assessment, is related to our instruction and objectives, and is a trustworthy indicator of student learning and development. Student assessment more frequently serves the purpose of awarding credits and grades (Milton, Pollio, and Eison, 1986) than the purpose of providing students with feedback that can improve their learning or providing instructors with feedback that can improve their teaching and courses (Loacker, 1988). One consequence of an overemphasis on grading is that students tend to view academic work through the "grade point average perspective" (Becker, Geer, and Hughes, 1968).

Student assessment and learning can and should be integrally related. Learning, in the broad sense, is both a process and an outcome, resulting in some qualitative change in knowledge, skills, attitudes, and/or values. Feedback resulting from both informal and formal means of student assessment can aid the learning process if that feedback is specific, timely, and on target with clear performance expectations. A test score or grade without such diagnostic feedback or explanation lacks completeness for the learner. Furthermore, frequent opportunities to perform and practice with informed and diagnostic feedback are usually necessary for novice learners to become more expert. The formative use of student assessment can help learners to become more proficient in their own self-assessments and in learning how to learn, as well as in acquiring substantive knowledge and skills (Study Group, 1984).

Similarly, faculty can improve their instructional performance through student assessment. The construction and use of student assessment measures is one of the most critical, yet underemphasized, instructional responsibilities of faculty. No matter what we say our expectations are for student performance, the instruments, procedures, and interpretations we use in student assessment constitute the operational objectives of our instruction. Significant gains can occur in the quality of our instruction when we make changes in our student assessment practices that are consistent with the learning outcomes we wish our students to attain and when we modify our instruction based on what we learn from student assessment. Student performance on carefully selected and developed assessment measures can provide important indicators of instructional practices that are relatively weak or strong. Along with other information, assessment results can help locate particular aspects of instruction that can be improved. In these respects, the quality of student assessment is closely associated with the quality of instruction that students actually experience (Loacker, 1988).

Faculty Assessment. Our disposition toward counting things and quantifying performance is often reflected in decisions about faculty involving promotion, tenure, and merit salary increases (Tuckman, 1976). Examples of the propensity to quantify performance include such measures as the number of published articles in particular refereed journals (indicator of research productivity), student ratings of instructors using Likert-type scales (indicator of teaching productivity), and the number of professional association and university committees served on (indicator of service productivity). The problem is not with these quantitative measures themselves. The problem is that quantitative evidence of faculty performance is susceptible to use independent of the objectives, substance, context, or other circumstances surrounding the tasks that faculty actually perform (Scriven, 1987). Furthermore, an overemphasis on quantifying performance can result in "bottom-line" calculations or comparisons that overlook the responsibilities, effort, and outcomes representing individual faculty members' contributions to their academic units.

With regard to formative feedback, faculty have reported generally receiving little (Davey and Sell, 1984, 1985). Prior to fourth-year or sixth-year reviews, new faculty may not have received any detailed and diagnostic feedback from colleagues or the department chairperson. Faculty claims that they are not sure of the basis on which their performance is judged or how their performance could be improved can sometimes be traced to omissions of sound personnel practices (Miller, 1987). Tenured faculty, especially full professors, sometimes do not seek or receive feedback that could improve their teaching, research, or service performance.

In most institutions, the front-line responsibilities for faculty assessment fall on the shoulders of department chairpersons, with faculty committees or the faculty at large contributing recommendations on which the chairpersons are expected to act. The role of the department chairperson in the assessment of faculty is reflected in two main responsibilities. One is to work with faculty in the assessment of colleagues (or prospective colleagues) and of their own performance. Another is to make judgments about the worth and merit of individual faculty for personnel decisions. A complicating factor is that chairpersons tend to walk a thin line between being a faculty colleague and being an administrator (Tucker, 1981).

The responsibilities of department chairpersons imply technical and interpersonal expertise, as well as legal savvy, associated with faculty assessment. Seldom are department chairpersons formally prepared or mentored for their complex roles in faculty development and evaluation. Acquiring knowledge and skills related to chairperson responsibilities for faculty assessment usually occurs on the job and through trial and error. Bennett (1983) illustrates some of these dilemmas and ambiguities faced by academic unit administrators.

Program Assessment. Program reviews may serve a wide range of purposes. When conducted for the purpose of external accreditation or recognition, they tend to be directed toward providing evidence of how well instruction, research, and/or service activities are performed, usually based on perceptions of quality (Conrad and Wilson, 1985). In this sense, not only is feedback for improvement underemphasized but also program weaknesses may be camouflaged or rationalized because of the sanctions they could bring.

External program reviews, similar to student and faculty assessments, often emphasize the quantitative aspects of performance. Examples of such quantitative measures of programs include: the number and high school background of students served; the standardized test scores of students who apply and are admitted; class size; the number of credit hours and grade point averages of students who take particular courses or who are majors in particular programs; the number or percent of undergraduates who are accepted to graduate school or who pass a certifying exam; the publication, citation, and grant record of faculty; the size and currency of physical facilities, equipment, and materials; and so forth. While important judgments about quality are embedded within these kinds of quantitative data, the underlying qualitative factors often must be unraveled and systematically examined in detail to reach a more profound understanding of program quality. Given these kinds of data normally collected and examined during program reviews, we should not be surprised that external program reviews lead to recommendations such as downsizing or eliminating programs, implementing or elevating selective admissions policies, expanding library holdings, updating physical facilities, and conducting more focused or larger research projects. Attention to the detailed and in-depth diagnosis of what and how programs could improve can be easily overlooked in assessments associated with program reviews.

When institutions establish their own form of internal program review, these reviews may be tied to budget decisions or designed to emphasize the improvement purpose of assessment. Using a combination of department and institutionwide representatives who concentrate on understanding how a program works and why, internal program reviews can, with proper arrangements, lead to action plans for improving academic performance (Arns and Poland, 1980). Furthermore, internal program reviews can help prepare for external reviews and provide information beyond the quantitative and comparative features of programs.

Institutional Assessment. Many of the comments about external program reviews can also be applied to institutional accreditation reviews, which are usually conducted by one of the regional accrediting associations. The process usually includes an institutional self-study, documentation of evidence responding to several prescribed issues, an on-site visit by a team of external reviewers, and a written report by the review team (North Central Association of Colleges and Schools, 1984). Since there is a relatively long time between institutional accreditation reviews and since such reviews for a complex institution are so vast, they may be perceived more as a formal procedure than as an instrumental undertaking that can result in significant changes for improvement. The recent emphasis of accrediting associations on evidence of student outcomes as part of institutional self-studies has the potential to change some institutional assessment practices, but this development is in an early stage, and its role in using assessment to improve performance is yet to be demonstrated.

The most common form of institutionwide assessment occurs through data bases that are regularly collected and updated. Colleges and universities have a long history of collecting institutional data that can serve a number of useful purposes. Examples of these purposes include recruiting, selecting, and placing students; making judgments about students, faculty, and program performance; forecasting and controlling income and expenditures; scheduling and servicing classroom facilities; and so forth.

However, potential users of institutional data bases may not know they exist, may not have access to them, or may not know how to access them. In some cases, institutions may not be collecting data that would be useful. In other cases, existing institutional data bases may have structural or technical defects, such as the lack of relational properties for linking or comparing two sets of data or the lack of conceptually sound and discrete data categories with explicit definitions of data elements.

Then, too, data that could be useful for institutional assessment are often mindlessly (that is, in a mechanical or routine manner) collected, stored, retrieved, analyzed, and reported. Sometimes mindlessness extends to the use of institutional data because of the form in which they are reported, the lack of contextual information, inadequate preparation of those who use the data, and so forth. For the most part, institutional data are reported and used in a summary fashion—that is, in gross detail and from one time period to the next. Relatively little attention is given to the diagnostic value of institutional data—that is, their use as indicators of what could be improved and what could be looked at in greater detail. Data-rich institutions can still be information poor because (1) the proper data are not available to the relevant users in a timely or convenient fashion, (2) data are viewed as power and access to them is strictly limited, (3) capabilities are lacking for organizing and translating data into useful information for particular audiences, uses, and circumstances, or any combination of these.

When we consider the breadth of student, faculty, program, and institutional assessment activities that colleges and universities undertake, with concomitant commitments of human and financial resources, there appear to be serious shortcomings in realizing the promises of assessment for improvement and development. An institution that effectively practices assessment for both improvement and accountability (including demands originating from sources outside the institution as well as decisions involving resource allocation, personnel decisions, certification, and so forth within the institution) is an ideal that few have realized. After a description of this ideal, some of the organizational realities that confront the practice of assessment are addressed, followed by a discussion of some strategies that could enhance the benefits of assessment.

A Model of the Ideal Self-Assessing Institution

Wildavsky (1972) has given considerable thought to the characteristics of institutions that have strong commitments to assessment. Although Wildavsky did not concentrate on any particular type of organization, the model he describes could be applied to colleges and universities. The ideal college or university, slightly adapted from Wildavsky's description, would have the following characteristics that cut across student, faculty, program, and institutional assessment:

1. Activities would be continuously monitored so as to determine whether goals were being met or even whether those goals should continue to prevail.

2. When assessment suggests that a change in goals or in the means to achieve them is desirable, these proposals would be taken seriously by those in the institution who could effect changes.

3. Organizational members would not have undue vested interests in the continuation of current activities; they would steadily pursue new alternatives to better serve the latest desired outcomes.

4. In some meaningful way, the entire institution would be infused with the assessment ethic, both for accountability and for improvement.

5. Assessments would result in the alteration or abolition of activities when the analyses indicate that changes are desirable.

6. All knowledge would be contingent, because improvement is always possible and change for the better is always in view though not necessarily yet attained.

7. Assumptions would be continuously challenged and reinforced by an attitude of scientific doubt rather than dogmatic commitment.

8. New truth would be sought rather than the defense of old norms and errors, and testing hypotheses would be essential to the main work of the institution.

9. The costs and benefits of alternative strategies (approaches, programs, policies) would be analyzed as precisely as available knowledge permits.

10. Assessments would be open, truthful, and explicit; conclusions would be publicly stated, showing how they were determined and giving others the opportunity to refute them; everything would be aboveboard, nothing would be hidden.

These characteristics of the self-assessing organization would seem on the surface to be entirely compatible with and reinforcing of the nature of academic pursuits in higher education institutions. However, does this model of the ideal assessing organization square with the needs of institutions and their individual members? Assuming that assessment is desirable, to what extent can we reasonably expect that colleges and universities will fully practice it? Which organizational characteristics might account for varying degrees of success with assessment, and how might these characteristics be changed?

Organizational Realities

As Wildavsky (1972) points out, the concepts of organization and assessment may be contradictory notions. At the institutional and academic unit levels, organization provides a structure that, among other things, offers stability for its members, generates and supports long-term commitments to the academic enterprise, and relates existing activities and programs to clientele and sponsors external to the university. Assessment, on the other hand, is an intervention that suggests change or at least the potential for change, that promotes skepticism and criticism, and that seeks to establish (and question) relationships among needs, objectives, and actions.

At the level of the individual faculty member and administrator, the potential conflict between assessment and individual needs is also apparent. The change threshold for individuals is limited. If assessment is forever challenging cherished beliefs and seeking to promote changes on a continuing basis, faculty and administrators could experience disabling stress and anxiety, finding it difficult to get their bearings and being in a quandary about what they should be doing. Continuing assessment activities could lead to severe individual hesitation or random behavior designed to cover as many bases as possible. Widespread confusion among faculty and administrators would produce unacceptable inefficiencies and adversely affect a necessary degree of cohesiveness and stability in academic units and central administration.

Beyond these general considerations, other more specific conditions are encountered in the assessment activities of higher education institutions. Attention is given here to six such organizational conditions that are viewed as restraining or tempering the practice of assessment.

Required Effort and Expertise. If faculty and administrators were fully involved in all aspects of assessment, there would be little time available for other responsibilities related to teaching, research, service, student advising, administration, and external relations. Needs for assessment must be balanced somehow with other institutional responsibilities.

Then, too, not everyone is equally qualified to perform all aspects of assessment. Effective assessment requires a mix of conceptual, technical, and interpersonal skills for which individual faculty and administrators may not be adequately prepared or experienced. Yet my assertion is that, to make formative and summative assessment most useful, faculty and administrators should be involved as practitioners of assessment and not just as passive recipients of assessment information.

Some of the organizational issues related to required effort and expertise for assessment include: To what extent will faculty and administrators be involved in assessment? Are assessment responsibilities considered as part of, or in addition to, ongoing tasks? How will faculty and administrators be supported and rewarded in their continuing professional development of assessment capabilities? If other people besides faculty and administrators will be involved with assessment, what will they be expected to do, with what authority, and in which realms (student, faculty, program, institution) of assessment activities? How will the responsibilities for assessment be divided among faculty administrators and staff, and to what extent will assessment be decentralized?

Costs and Benefits. Resources used for assessment are part of institutional costs, and incremental assessment activities add to institutional costs. On the other hand, existing or new assessment practices can produce benefits not only for satisfying accountability requirements but also for meeting the continuing development needs of students, faculty, programs, and the institution itself.

There is little evidence in the literature that trade-offs between the costs and benefits of various kinds of assessment have been systematically examined (Halpern, 1987). For example, do institutions have a reasonable fix on the cost of student assessment that occurs as a regular part of testing and grading within courses? Have institutions examined what benefits are associated with current assessment practices? Do institutions have any baseline for comparing either the benefits or costs of assessment alternatives?

Ewell and Jones (1986) sidestep these issues in favor of exploring incremental or marginal costs associated with adding new assessment activities, primarily student assessment instruments (tests and surveys) administered at the institution-wide level. They consider the direct costs of instruments constructed locally or purchased from an outside vendor, of administration of the instruments, of instrument scoring and data analysis, and of coordination of the assessment effort. Taking four different types of institutions (private liberal arts college, major public university, comprehensive regional university, and community college), Ewell and Jones construct four sets of institutional cost estimates based on student samples within each kind of institution. Their cost estimates show a range of approximately $29,000 to $130,000 for an annual student assessment program limited to quantifiable indicators within relatively constricted measures of student development. Assuming for the moment the accuracy of these cost estimates, we can see that student assessment (not to mention other aspects of faculty, program, or institutional assessment) can add significantly to institutional costs. These incremental requirements for assessment compete with other institutional priorities for attention and, for most institutions, do so without reference to other ongoing assessment costs or the current and potential benefits from these investments.

In addition to direct and indirect costs for assessment, there are likely to be opportunity costs since attention to assessment could reduce or eliminate effort devoted to other productive activities. Perhaps equally or even more significant, there are additional costs of changes linked to the assessment process and its results. As with other initiatives, a university or college will be limited in the resources it can allocate for assessment and the changes associated with it.

The main point here is that the various costs of assessment should be carefully considered in relation to the actual and potential benefits. Assessment can have both positive and negative effects as well as intended, unintended, and unanticipated outcomes (see Conrad and Wilson, 1985, for a discussion of the possible differences between outcomes and effects). Just as not all change is for the better, not all assessment is for the better. A thorough and continuing examination of the costs and benefits of assessment (current and proposed practices) would seem to be an organizational imperative.

External Support. If the survival and vitality of institutions is dependent, in large part, on the supply of resources (financial, human, and so forth) from their environments (Pfeffer and Salancik, 1978) and if a college or university is not strongly committed to particular programs, clientele, and sponsors (one of the qualities of the self-assessing organization), it may be unreasonable to expect that assessments will lead to the building of external support (although assessment may be required as a condition for funding or accreditation). Furthermore, if one requirement of an organization is to adapt to its environment, it may also be unreasonable to expect that administrators and faculty will select priorities and programs that are based primarily on internal assessments and their justification. Faculty and administrators, for reasons of both self-interest and institutional interest, may interpret and use assessment results with a view toward receiving external support and achieving some relatively high degree of success. The ideals of a higher education institution as a self-assessing organization become suspect, however, if faculty and administrators (1) seek out problems that are easy to solve and changes that are easy to make because they do not require radical departures from the past, (2) hold back assessment information until the time is propitious for its release, or (3) seize an opportunity whether or not the assessments are completed or justified. All of these conditions limit the potential of assessment in colleges and universities.

Internal Politics. Assessments may be wielded as a weapon in institutional wars—that is, they may be used by one party against another or for one cause, policy, or program against another. When this happens, assessment becomes much less than an ideal organizational characteristic as described by Wildavsky (1972). The assessment enterprise depends on a common recognition and respect that the activity is being carried out in order to secure better programs and practices, whatever these may be, and not to support a predetermined position or decision.

Equilibrium and Stress. As with other organizations, higher education institutions require some balance between efforts that provide stability and those that induce changes. If those involved in assessments try to do too much—that is, undertake initiatives that lead to sustained and widespread organizational changes—they risk failure in maintaining a "vote of confidence." If they try to do too little, they risk abandoning their own beliefs and losing the support of their most dedicated followers. The strains of maintaining a balance between change and stability are not easy for those dedicated to assessment. Likewise, the dissemination of assessment information can cause negative side effects that create instability in the organization. If assessment information shows how badly off an institution, program, faculty, or student body is compared to what it ought to be, this can create (or accelerate) paranoia, distrust, or general dissatisfaction detrimental to the college or university and its constituencies.

Rewards and Disincentives. In the ideal situation, the assessment ethic would be infused throughout the institution and would be equitably rewarded. Other considerations (such as required effort, financial implications, external image, internal politics, and stability) can often prevail, however, over assessment initiatives and their results. Furthermore, if assessments are accepted when they lead to a reduction in required resources and rejected when they require increases in expenditures, individuals and organizational units are likely to withhold information or selectively offer information to protect themselves. As Wildavsky (1972) aptly summarizes, "it's the same the whole world over: The analytically virtuous are not necessarily rewarded nor are the wicked (who do not evaluate) punished" (p. 515).

Making Assessment Effective

In view of the organizational realities of most colleges and universities, it is possible to practice effective assessment within some reasonable constraints and expectations. Some actions that administrators and faculty could take are discussed next.

Involve Individuals and Offices with Recognized Authority, Leadership, and Expertise. Wildavsky (1972) observes: "If evaluation is not done at all, if it is done but not used, if used but twisted out of shape, the place to look first is not the technical apparatus but the organization [itself]" (p. 518). Two important features of college and university organization that are necessary for a viable assessment enterprise are recognized authority and leadership with expertise.

Authority is legitimated power (French and Raven, 1968). One approach to attaining such authority for the assessment function is to institutionalize it in some manner. While the ideal institutionalization of assessment is to diffuse and embed it in activities throughout a college or university, a more common approach is to establish one (centralized) or several (decentralized) units or offices within the institution to spearhead this function. The institutionalization of assessment requires resource commitments that involve a dependable flow of resources beyond one-shot studies. Adequate financial resources for assessment activities, with their associated accountability, might be allocated to established units, such as offices of institutional research, planning, evaluation, or program review; new offices or units charged with the specific mission of assessment or some subset of assessment activities; or external assessors or firms who conduct specific studies for the institution and report to a designated office, committee, or administrator. Whichever arrangements are made for the institutionalization of assessment, the works of Clark (1987) and others have underscored the importance of "organizational culture," especially faculty norms and values, in establishing and maintaining institutional support. The faculty role in staffing and governing the assessment function, wherever it is located, is a critical consideration for its legitimization. A blend of administrative, collegial, and individual authority (Bess, 1988) will probably be necessary for the effective performance of assessment activities in colleges and universities.

The leadership requirement for assessment has at least three dimensions. First, leadership is needed in the form of advocacy for assessment. Without strong and influential advocates for assessment, adequate resources and other forms of authority are not likely to be available. Second, leadership is required in the practice of assessment. If we assume that proper assessment requires both expertise and dedicated effort, relating assessment activities to the most important concerns of faculty, academic units, and central offices is a significant leadership task. Arrangements for the support and reward of those engaged in assessment is also associated with this leadership task. Third, leadership is needed in the allocation and use of computer technology for assessment. Two particular kinds of expertise for technology-related assessment activities are becoming more evident. These are the design and development of academic information systems that conveniently link data to the tasks that faculty and administrators perform and the translation of data into information and knowledge that is useful for particular audiences and purpose. The potential of assessment activities to support organizational inquiry is closely linked to the effective use of computer technology (Fincher, 1985; Rohrbaugh and McCartt, 1986).

Undertake Affordable Assessments That Demonstrate Effects. If one of the deficiencies of ineffective organizations is that they do not learn well from their experiences, an effective organization seeks to inquire into its experiences and to organize related information so that knowledge can be gained from these experiences (Mandelbaum, 1979). The most important part of this process is to select organizational questions that are worthy of pursuit and that are susceptible to some form of disciplined inquiry within available resources. In other words, assessment activities must be affordable while addressing questions and issues of significance to the quality and effectiveness of the institution. Cameron (1987) provides a conceptual framework for examining literature on the quality and effectiveness of higher education institutions.

Assessments and their results should also be more than a set of good ideas without a notion of how they can be implemented. The proof of a good idea is that it works when tried, realizing that implementation may require a number of trials, errors, and their associated learnings. The implementation of new assessment practices, as well as changes resulting from assessment activities, may depend on the ability of those who produce the changes to make others (including those outside the institution and clients) pay for the associated costs. If the change makers are themselves forced to bear the financial brunt of their actions, they are likely to become conservative and try to stabilize their environment (Wildavsky,

1972). This all suggests that some slack resources may be required within the institution for assessment practices to be effective.

In addition, the selection, design, and use of assessments should be informed by the diagnosis of costs and benefits associated with current and alternative courses of action. An examination of the cost-effectiveness or cost-benefit of assessment alternatives should include the immediate resources and effects attributed to particular practices as well as the longer-term ones.

Maintain Discretion, Diversity, and Flexibility. Assessments that become public and reveal findings or promote changes that are perceived as detrimental to institutional constituencies are likely to be rejected by them. In addition, assessment information should be always treated with sensitivity and discretion.

Just as diversity of programs can enable institutions to be more responsive to a range of problems and clientele, a similar case could be built for the diversity of assessment practices. Placing all of the assessment eggs in one methodological basket—such as standardized instruments or informal ways of assessing student outcomes—is not a sound strategy for any institution. Neither is it sound practice for an institution to emphasize only one dimension of assessment (for example, the cognitive development of students in quantitative reasoning or the lecture performance of faculty in multimethod courses) to the exclusion of other dimensions that are necessary to understand and enrich the meaning of particular findings. Again, some reasonable balance should be sought between being spread too thinly across assessment methods and topics and concentrating attention on only one area. Teaching and learning and the environments that influence them are complex phenomena that require suitably matched approaches to assessment. Being wed to only one approach or area of assessment not only limits the realms of understanding but also constrains the ability of the institution to shift its assessment strategy.

Form Internal Coalitions and Cooperative Endeavors. Institutional assessment activities, in the broad view, are political in the sense of policy or program advocacy. "Without a steady source of political support . . . [assessment] will suffer the fate of abandoned children" (Wildavsky, 1972, p. 515). In addition, effective assessment is simply not possible without adequate data that can be turned into useful and timely information. To secure data from various sources, assessment activities require cooperation. The incentives (or potential gains) for cooperation must outweigh the disincentives (or potential losses).

Building support for assessment and related concerns in the institution usually requires some internal selling and, frequently, the formation of coalitions or special-interest groups. However, "political muscle" within colleges and universities must be exercised cautiously and within the rules for exercising power (more precisely, authority or legitimated power) with respect to particular decisions and decision-making processes. University policies, faculty rules, governance structures, and administrative procedures each play a part in shaping the arena in which decisions related to assessment are made and implemented. In addition, as noted earlier, the culture of colleges and universities—often characterized by faculty autonomy, academic freedom, discipline affiliations and specializations, and decentralization of authority—plays a powerful role in shaping decisions and decision-making processes (Clark, 1987).

Attend to Institutional Characteristics and Readiness to Change in Assessment Design and Implementation. Assessments of student outcomes, general education curricula, or faculty performance can occur without regard to the particular characteristics of a college or university or its readiness to support assessment initiatives. However, unless key organizational factors are anticipated and accommodated or changed in assessment activities, it is highly unlikely that existing assessment practices will be altered or made more effective. Examples of organizational features of colleges and universities that should be examined for their changeability in relationship to assessment activities and findings include: institutional mission, priorities, and diversity of programs; course schedules and offerings; instructional formats and approaches; academic calendars; space and equipment restrictions; budgeting processes and financial resources available; faculty assignments and workloads; student selection, enrollment, and graduation requirements; collective bargaining agreements (if applicable); and so forth.

Assessment can be adapted to particular organizational characteristics as well as serve as an organizational change agent. Both individual and organizational changes are potentially involved in implementing assessment practices. The success of assessment may depend on readiness to change—that is, readiness to accept certain assessment practices or to implement recommendations growing out of assessment findings. When individual faculty members or administrators are the focus, readiness for change can involve a combination of attitudes, values, beliefs, skills, and knowledge about assessment and its uses. When organizational units and the total organization are the focus, readiness for change can involve a combination of structures, rewards, norms, resources, and policies that bear on assessment (Abedor and Sachs, 1978).

Those involved in deliberations about undertaking new assessment initiatives could profitably address the following issues: Is the institution (faculty, students, administrators, support staff, trustees) prepared to undertake new assessment practices with reasonable expectations for success? What can be done to prepare individuals and organizational units for a proposed change in assessment? How can assessment practices accommodate needs for individual and organizational stability while providing evidence for changes that can lead to improvements?

Build Community That Values Assessment. One of the most fundamental steps for colleges and universities wishing to upgrade their assessment practices is to ascertain whether prevalent values in the institution support the notion of assessment and, if not, what can be done to develop support. Two shared values, in particular, are directly related to the effective practice of assessment.

One value is an orientation toward experimentation and reasonable risk taking. Experiments are necessary for testing hypotheses and relating goals and objectives to results in the context of limited resources. In this sense, a college or university is a natural laboratory for experimentation and for assessment aimed at the improvement of performance.

Cooperation and collaboration comprise a second shared value essential to an effective assessment program. If the primary orientation of faculty and administrators is that organizational members (and units) are competing for a fixed pie of limited resources and if information about individuals and units is a powerful source to be protected, then collaboration within and across groups is likely to be limited. If, however, the primary orientation is that the pie of organizational resources can expand and that the performance of individuals and units is interdependent, then there is a much more positive environment for cooperation in assessment activities. Astin (1985) discusses these and other issues related to values that underlie concepts of quality in higher education.

The sense of trust among individuals and groups underlies cooperative acts beneficial to assessment activities. The credibility and equitability of assessment activities can, in turn, build trust that promotes cooperation and an experimental attitude. However, more assessment information alone will not necessarily lead to greater agreement or collaboration if the institution is wracked by fundamental differences in values. Assessment need not create agreement, but it may presuppose agreement (Wildavsky, 1972).

Conclusion

I do not wish to play down the importance of student outcomes assessment. It is terribly important, is often not adequately attended to, and should be vigorously and thoughtfully pursued on each college and university campus. Beginning with work initiated almost two decades ago at the Western Interstate Commission for Higher Education (Lawrence, Weathersby, and Patterson, 1970) and extended through current work at the National Center for Higher Education Management Systems (NCHEMS) under the leadership of Peter Ewell and Dennis Jones, I have been both an observer and participant in the formative stages of the assessment movement. For example, the NCHEMS student outcomes structure was applied in my work on adult and continuing education with the late

John Putnam at the National Center for Education Statistics (Putnam and Sell, 1983). I have also been fortunate for nearly the past ten years to be located at an institution that has provided "hands-on" experiences with student assessment as a teacher, researcher, consultant, and administrator for an office of instructional development and evaluation. All of these experiences have enhanced, not reduced, my sense of the importance of student outcomes assessment.

What I have tried to emphasize in this chapter is the organizational context and forces within colleges and universities that inhibit as well as nurture assessment in its many forms. I have tried to say that student outcomes assessment is never separate from other institutional issues, is affected and used by other kinds of assessment activities, and should be carefully examined for its avowed purposes, actual uses, and consequences. Throughout this chapter I have pleaded a case for balance—of the purposes that assessment serves, of methodological approaches and foci for assessment, of effort given to assessment and other critical activities, and of response to external concerns while continuing to develop and improve individual and organizational performance.

I wish to conclude on an upbeat note. The outlook for the future of higher education and for the contribution of assessment to that future has never been brighter. With the possible exception of the late 1960s and early 1970s, higher education is more visible and more widely discussed today than in any preceding period. All kinds of audiences and stakeholders have high expectations for colleges and universities and the models and benefits that they provide for other segments of society.

I believe that most institutions are becoming highly sophisticated in dealing with a variety of assessment issues. Many of these assessment issues will continue into the next decade, but some new challenges and opportunities will also present themselves. If we are able to balance and meet the competing needs for our attention and to use assessment for enhancing the worth of individuals as well as our institutions, we will be on our way toward building strong colleges and universities for the twenty-first century.

References

Abedor, A. J., and Sachs, S. G. "The Relationship Between Faculty Development, Organizational Development, and Instructional Development: Readiness for Instructional Innovation in Higher Education." In R. K. Bass and D. B. Lumsden (eds.), *Instructional Development: The State of the Art.* Columbus, Ohio: Collegiate Publishing, 1978.

Adelman, C. *Assessment in Higher Education.* Washington, D.C.: Office of Educational Research and Improvement, U.S. Department of Education, 1986.

Arns, R. G., and Poland, W. "Changing the University Through Program Review." *Journal of Higher Education,* 1980, *51* (3), 268–285.

Astin, A. W. *Achieving Educational Excellence: A Critical Assessment of Priorities and Practices in Higher Education.* San Francisco: Jossey-Bass, 1985.

Baldridge, J. V. *Power and Conflict in the University.* New York: Wiley, 1971.

Barak, R. J. *Program Review in Higher Education: Within and Without.* Boulder, Colo.: National Center for Higher Education Management Systems, 1982.

Barak, R. J. "The Role of Program Review in Strategic Planning." *Association for Institutional Research Professional File,* 1986, *26,* 4-7.

Becker, H. S., Geer, B., and Hughes, E. C. *Making the Grade: The Academic Side of College Life.* New York: Wiley, 1968.

Beidler, P. G. (ed.). *Distinguished Teachers on Effective Teaching: Observations on Teaching by College Professors Recognized by the Council for Advancement and Support of Education.* New Directions for Teaching and Learning, no. 28. San Francisco: Jossey-Bass, 1986.

Bennett, J. B. *Managing the Academic Department: Cases and Notes.* New York: American Council on Education, 1983.

Bennett, J. B., and Chater, S. S. "Evaluating the Performance of Tenured Faculty Members." *Educational Record,* 1984, *65,* 38-41.

Bess, J. L. *Collegiality and Bureaucracy in the Modern University.* New York: Teachers College, Columbia University, 1988.

Blau, P. M. *The Organization of Academic Work.* New York: Wiley, 1973.

Cameron, K. S. "Improving Academic Quality and Effectiveness." In M. W. Peterson (ed.), *Key Resources on Higher Education Governance, Management, and Leadership: A Guide to the Literature.* San Francisco: Jossey-Bass, 1987.

Centra, J. A. *Determining Faculty Effectiveness: Assessing Teaching, Research, and Service for Personnel Decisions and Improvement.* San Francisco: Jossey-Bass, 1979.

Clark, B. R. *The Academic Life: Small Worlds, Different Worlds.* Princeton, N.J.: Princeton University Press, 1987.

Cohen, M. D., and March, J. G. *Leadership and Ambiguity.* New York: McGraw-Hill, 1974.

Conrad, C. F., and Wilson, R. F. *Academic Program Review: Institutional Approaches, Expectations, and Controversies.* ASHE-ERIC Higher Education Report, no. 5. Washington, D.C.: Association for the Study of Higher Education, 1985.

Davey, K. B., and Sell, G. R. "The Role Evaluation Could Play in Improving and Developing Instructional Excellence in a Doctoral-Granting University." Paper presented at the joint meeting of the Evaluation Research Society and Evaluation Network, San Francisco, October 11, 1984.

Davey, K. B., and Sell, G. R. "Instructional Evaluation for Development/Improvement: Fact or Fiction Based on a Case Study of Faculty Practices?" Paper presented at the annual meeting of the American Educational Research Association, Chicago, April 1, 1985.

Ewell, P. T. (ed.). *Assessing Educational Outcomes.* New Directions for Institutional Research, no. 47. San Francisco: Jossey-Bass, 1985.

Ewell, P. T., and Jones, D. P. "The Costs of Assessment." In C. Adelman (ed.), *Assessment in Higher Education.* Washington, D.C.: Office of Educational Research and Improvement, U.S. Department of Education, 1986.

Fincher, C. "The Art and Science of Institutional Research." In M. W. Peterson and M. Corcoran (eds.), *Institutional Research in Transition.* New Directions for Institutional Research, no. 46. San Francisco: Jossey-Bass, 1985.

French, R. P., and Raven, B. "The Bases of Social Power." In D. Cartwright and A. Zander (eds.), *Group Dynamics: Research and Theory.* (3rd ed.) New York: Harper & Row, 1968.

Halpern, D. F. (ed.). *Student Outcomes Assessment: What Institutions Stand to Gain.* New Directions for Higher Education, no. 59. San Francisco: Jossey-Bass, 1987.

Hartle, T. W. "The Growing Interest in Measuring the Educational Achievement of College Students." In C. Adelman (ed.), *Assessment in Higher Education.* Washington, D.C.: Office of Educational Research and Improvement, U.S. Department of Education, 1986.

Lawrence, B., Weathersby, G., and Patterson, V. W. *Outputs of Higher Education: Their Identification, Measurement, and Evaluation.* Boulder, Colo.: Western Interstate Commission for Higher Education, 1970.

Lawrence, J. K., and Green, K. C. *A Question of Quality: The Higher Education Ratings Game.* AAHE-ERIC Higher Education Report, no. 5. Washington, D.C.: American Association for Higher Education, 1980.

Licata, C. M. *Posttenure Faculty Evaluation: Threat or Opportunity.* ASHE-ERIC Higher Education Report, no. 1. Washington, D.C.: Association for the Study of Higher Education, 1986.

Loacker, G. "Faculty as a Force to Improve Instruction Through Assessment." In J. H. McMillan (ed.), *Assessing Students' Learning.* New Directions for Teaching and Learning, no. 34. San Francisco: Jossey-Bass, 1988.

McMillan, J. H. (ed.). *Assessing Students' Learning.* New Directions for Teaching and Learning. no. 34. San Francisco: Jossey-Bass, 1988.

Mandelbaum, S. J. "The Intelligence of Universities." *Journal of Higher Education,* 1979, *50* (6), 697-725.

Micek, S. S. (ed.). *Integrating Academic Planning and Budgeting in a Rapidly Changing Environment.* Boulder, Colo.: National Center for Higher Education Management Systems, 1980.

Miller, R. I. *Evaluating Faculty for Promotion and Tenure.* San Francisco: Jossey-Bass, 1987.

Millett, J. D. *The Academic Community.* New York: McGraw-Hill, 1962.

Millett, J. D. *New Structures of Campus Power: Success and Failures of Emerging Forms of Institutional Governance.* San Francisco: Jossey-Bass, 1978.

Milton, O., Pollio, H. R., and Eison, J. A. *Making Sense of College Grades: Why the Grading System Does Not Work and What Can Be Done About It.* San Francisco: Jossey-Bass, 1986.

North Central Association of Colleges and Schools. *A Handbook of Accreditation.* Chicago: Commission on Institutions of Higher Education, North Central Association of Colleges and Schools, 1984.

Ohio Board of Regents. *Developing a Process Model for Institutional and State-Level Review and Evaluation of Academic Programs.* Columbus: Ohio Board of Regents, 1979.

Pfeffer, J., and Salancik, G. R. *The External Control of Organizations: A Resource-Dependence Perspective.* New York: Harper & Row, 1978.

Putnam, J. F., and Sell, G. R. *Adult Learning Activities: A Handbook of Terminology for Classifying and Describing the Learning Activities of Adults.* Washington, D.C.: National Center for Education Statistics, 1983.

Rohrbaugh, J., and McCartt, A. T. (eds.). *Applying Decision Support Systems in Higher Education.* New Directions for Institutional Research, no. 49. San Francisco: Jossey-Bass, 1986.

Schalock, H. D., and Sell, G. R. "A Framework for the Analysis and Empirical Investigation of Educational RDD&E." In H. D. Schalock and G. R. Sell (eds.), *The Oregon Studies in Educational Research, Development, Diffusion, and Evaluation (RDD&E): Conceptual Frameworks.* Monmouth, Ore.: Teaching Research, A Division of the Oregon State System of Higher Education, 1971.

Scriven, M. "Validity in Personnel Evaluation." *Journal of Personnel Evaluation in Education,* 1987, *1* (1), 9-23.

Shirley, R. C., and Volkwein, J. F. "Establishing Academic Program Priorities." *Journal of Higher Education,* 1978, *49* (5), 472-489.

Study Group on the Conditions of Excellence in American Higher Education. *Involvement in Learning: Realizing the Potential of American Higher Education.* Washington, D.C.: National Institute of Education, 1984.

Tucker, A. *Chairing the Academic Department: Leadership Among Peers.* Washington, D.C.: American Council on Education, 1981.

Tuckman, H. P. *Publication, Teaching, and the Academic Reward Structure.* Lexington, Mass.: Heath, 1976.

Wildavsky, A. "The Self-Evaluating Organization." *Public Administration Review,* 1972, *32* (5), 509-520.

G. Roger Sell is senior program director for organizational development in the Center for Teaching Excellence at The Ohio State University.

Good assessment is not something that is done to *someone; good assessment begins with commitment, not control.*

So, What's the Use?

Larry A. Braskamp

In my research on and practice in assessment and evaluation for the past twenty years, the most penetrating and challenging question I have been asked from clients and potential users is simply, "So?"—a shortcut for "So what?," which, in turn, is short for "What do the data mean, and therefore what should we do?" Every issue regarding the use of assessment emanates from this terse query. Often this question is asked after the assessment data are in the hands of the potential audiences, indicating clearly that the assessment's usefulness had not previously been given adequate attention.

There are many different answers to the question of "So, what's the use?" A typical one goes like this: "We assess to demonstrate that we in higher education are responsible stewards of resources and to assist us in improving what we currently do." While the first, summative use cannot and should not be avoided, it must not be the sole use if assessment is to reach its potential as an administrative and instructional activity. However, use for improvement is often a vague goal and does specifically guide the practice of assessment. In this chapter I try to describe some guidelines for planning and implementing assessment for improvement, using my views of effective institutions as the context for determining the value of assessment. In short, when is the practice of assessment effective and useful?

An effective institution is one that simultaneously fosters the development of its members (for example, faculty) and fulfills its shared collective objectives (Braskamp and Krug, 1989). This definition is similar to that of others who study organizational effectiveness (Hackman, 1986; Lawler, 1986). It emphasizes the individual as well as the organization. Both the individual and the institution need to be considered in determining whether or not any administrative policy or practice is worthwhile and effective. Starting from this broad perspective allows us to develop some guidelines about how we should organize assessment programs for maximum usefulness.

Much of the rationale for assessment has been based on improved student performance, although assessment can also influence faculty behavior. Based on our research using the theory of personal investment (a motivational theory) to study workplace-related influences on employee productivity and work attitudes (Maehr and Braskamp, 1986), we argue that leaders in an organization engage in three major types of activities: (1) They define and communicate a mission, (2) they assess work performance, and (3) they recognize and involve employees (Braskamp and Krug, 1989). Thus, assessment is a major activity in enhancing organizational functioning. Like anything else, it can be used effectively or detrimentally; it can empower the members of the institution and keep the institution on course, or it can become an expensive and demoralizing bureaucratic undertaking. Therefore, the practice of assessment should also focus on its impact on the faculty and staff because they are some of the primary users and are ultimately responsible for determining the quality of the institution.

In summary, in order to answer the question, "So, what's the use?," institutions must address the purpose and context of assessment, keeping in mind the dual complementary goals of an effective organization—individual growth and well-being, as well as the achievement of collective goals.

Guidelines

In this section, I submit five guidelines that should be considered in designing and implementing an assessment program on any campus.

Determine the Focus. The first guideline for maximizing utilization of assessment by the faculty as a primary user is to determine the extent to which assessment is internal or intrinsic to the task itself. For example, if professors design learning assignments whereby student mastery of the assignments is evident to both the students and the instructor, the instructors automatically know the results of their teaching efforts. Professors may frequently give problem sets, short quizzes, or ask students to describe to them where they are having difficulty mastering the intended learning outcomes. If assessment is immediate and private, the users can claim ownership of the data produced and perceive the data as their own. Because of this sense of ownership, the chances of stakeholders accepting and acting on assessment information increases. Furthermore, intrinsic feedback from a performance such as teaching can influence future performance in a very positive way. This is a guiding principle in teaching students and should also be a principle in assessing teaching. A person can feel good about doing a job well and by doing it well can gain confidence in mastering more difficult and challenging tasks.

Cross (1988) has consistently reminded us that assessment, when viewed as a "large-scale testing program conducted at institutional or state levels to determine what students have learned in college," essentially misses the mark. Assessment to be useful needs to get into the classroom, the "scene of the action in education." If the ultimate purpose of assessment is improvement, we need to develop better linkages with those most responsible for what we are assessing—namely, the faculty responsible for the student learning. And the activity of assessment is everybody's business, not only those with expertise or an interest.

One practical way to check the condition of being intrinsic or internal is to ask faculty and staff two questions: (1) Do you collect information about the quality of your work solely for your own use? (2) If you do, do you share it with someone else? If the majority of those on any campus cannot say yes to these questions, I have limited confidence that any existing or proposed formalized assessment program will contribute much to fostering individual development and meeting institutional objectives.

Determine the Perceived Consequences. A second guideline relates to the perceived purpose of the information. Is assessment a way to raise self-awareness of strengths and shortcomings for individual or program development or to exercise external control in order to meet organizational goals? The former view is less threatening and more apt to facilitate the emergence and maintenance of interest in and motivation for the work itself. Assessment can also promote self-development. In the controlling view, on the other hand, assessment is perceived as a means of demonstrating accountability, usually from the top down. For example, if an institution decides to initiate an assessment program for use in the promotion and tenure process or to obtain more funding, the message of control will be quite clear unless the purpose of encouraging development is given equal public weight. Controversy and arguments against the nature of assessment will probably overshadow its constructive use.

This guideline deals with how assessment is viewed by its audiences. Assessment yields information that has power and influence in any organization. It is particularly important that faculty view assessment as a tool for their own personal growth more than as a necessary and evil chore that allows the institution to judge them. For example, viewing assessment of faculty only in terms of promotion and tenure or gains in student knowledge on a test to meet some external standard tends to focus on institutional control rather than to enhance faculty commitment. To be effective, assessment should be forward rather than backward looking. Feedback is to be used primarily to improve future performance.

Institutions should ask their faculty if they view feedback from assessment as informational rather than as controlling. Do the data primarily help the faculty or help someone else? Does assessment encompass not holding errors against someone as well as the necessity of passing judgment? Are honest mistakes or failures accepted as a part of trying and exploring?

Make Assessment Practices Participatory. When a person plays a role in establishing goals for the tasks to be performed and the standards of acceptable performance, investment in accomplishing the tasks increases (Mento, Steele, and Karren, 1987). Common goal setting is also a good way for people to learn about organizational expectations and to identify what they need from the organization in order to meet those expectations.

Ownership influences a person's sense of having control of his or her destiny. A sense of ownership is needed for a sense of identity and self-respect. Without this sense, a faculty member would have little reason to want to develop and make a contribution to the overall effectiveness of the institution. However, there is a potential danger to ownership; it can replace environmental pressures and demands. Tension may be reduced, but so is the necessity to be creative, to solve problems, and to solicit input from others and engage in cooperative ventures. Consequently, complacency may emerge, and complacency is often the enemy of excellence.

Recognize Faculty and Staff Differences. Based on our studies of faculty at research universities versus those at smaller teaching-oriented colleges, university faculty place greater value on striving for professional accomplishments while small-college faculty regard social concern for others as being more important (Maehr and Braskamp, 1986). If assessment practices are to facilitate faculty growth and development as well as student growth and development, the strategies should be designed to take into account the individual differences of the staff as well as the institutional goals of accountability. For example, if assessment looks only at professional excellence achieved through individual, independent efforts, then the impact of assessment on enhancing teamwork and cooperative ventures is likely to be minimal.

Make Suggestions for Improvement Part of Assessment. Feedback will more readily influence behavior if it includes alternatives and suggestions for change. Based on studies of faculty receiving student-rating information intended to improve instruction, we know that we can significantly improve teaching when consultation accompanies the results.

Faculty often know that they should improve and desire to do so, but they do not know how. Consultation that provides advice, suggestions, and alternatives for change needs to be presented as part of the assessment process. Schön (1983) suggests that professionals can improve their skills through "reflections-in-action," defined as "thinking about what they are doing while they are doing it" (p. xi). He advocates that this process should not be done in isolation. Instead, he notes that we learn by receiving coaching and using models in our efforts to become better professionals.

In sum, assessment can be effective if properly designed and implemented. Feedback needs to be integral and intrinsic to the work or task itself and not only an add-on activity to be used by others for control. Assessment requires the active participation of each person, with feedback including suggestions for change as a key component. Assessment must be done within an atmosphere of trust, respect for individual differences, and the freedom to fail. Assessment must provide benefits to participants; that is, they must feel they will receive external rewards in the form of salary increases and recognition as well as an increased sense of worth. Finally, personal characteristics may affect one's response to assessment. Those with "growth needs" or personal incentives to excel are more apt to gain from feedback. In short, to assess is to do more than to judge; it is to build.

Implications

The conditions for maximum utility of assessment just described provide some general guidelines for how best to conduct assessments in higher education settings. The following implications for an assessment program on a campus are based on these guidelines, but they also reflect my experiences in administering and using assessment programs.

An Assessment Program Reflects the Institutional Culture of a Campus. Assessment practices are powerful indicators of how an institution encourages its members to achieve excellence. They are potent tools for socializing people into the academic community. Faculty new to a local academic community use evaluation feedback to learn not only of their progress but also of institutional expectations and standards. How these expectations and feedback are communicated vary immensely from campus to campus. For example, the use of formal and legalistic procedures in which achievements are weighted by formula for their importance in judging a faculty member's worth conveys a different idea of what being a member of the community means than the use of evaluation practices within a mentoring program. Assessment can denote control and judgment only, or it can communicate a commitment to the community and to the growth and development of each member. In both cases, standards of excellence can be demanding: the difference lies in how they are communicated and in the link between the communication and the provision of explicit support to enable a member to achieve the desired ends. The question to ask the campus leaders is: How are your practices helping to build your institution?

The Goal of Assessment Is Self-Assessment. Professional people by definition are accountable and responsible for their own behavior. Assessment needs to promote rather than decrease this sense of responsibility. Thus, faculty members should learn to monitor their own behaviors, to make changes when necessary, to be more aware of institutional as well as of their own personal standards, and to link assessment with improvement. Any assessment program will last only if there is trust, credibility, respect, and autonomy for each individual member of the institution. Assessment by an institution is a balancing act, taking into account both individual needs and desires as well as the institution's responsibility to its constituencies, such as taxpayers, alumni, students, and funding agencies. Accountability thus works both ways: Each individual is accountable to the institution, but the institution also has a responsibility to each and every member. To accomplish this dual responsibility, I am advocating a self-assessing organization (Wildavsky, 1972). But, in doing so, I recognize the contradictory notions of organization and assessment, as discussed by Sell in Chapter Two. A proper balance is necessary if assessment is to contribute fully to the attainment of the dual complimentary goals of an organization.

Is Everybody's Business Everybody's Business? In an informal meeting, Robert Stake, a pioneer in the field of education evaluation, recently cautioned a small group of us about the promotion of the interconnectedness of our society, in which assessment becomes one important vehicle. We often think that full and complete disclosure and participation will solve our problems or make people more accountable. I advocate high participation and open exchanges, but we need to realize that this interconnectedness has a price attached to it. Stake argues that the burden of demonstrating that assessment practices have benefits that outweigh costs to the faculty rests with administrators. Moreover, it should be a stern obligation. Thus, before we in academia design elaborate assessment programs, we need to consider such issues as privacy and the need to know. Earlier I argued that assessment is everybody's business; however, one person's assessment business does not necessarily have to be everybody else's assessment business.

Any University Is Not a Just Place; It Is Just a Place. A former vice-chancellor for academic affairs often repeated this advice: "Remember, life is not fair, and you just have to accept that." It did not mean to him or to us that we should not try to be just or fair in our work but only that we need to recognize the imperfections and inequities that do and will exist. We simply cannot afford to become overwhelmed or cynical about it. This advice has been particularly salient in my working with faculty and administrators on designing assessment programs. Often our initial idealism for a new approach only leads to disappointment after implementation. Evaluating is fundamentally a human endeavor, and human imperfections only become more obvious when we are judging and helping others.

Assessment Practices Should Be Diverse and Flexible. There is no single best method to assess performance, just as there is no single best way to teach or conduct research. A diversity of approaches is needed. In evaluating teaching, we have advocated the multiple-perspective approach in which information about teaching effectiveness is obtained from a variety of sources—for example, faculty, peers, students, alumni, and self—using a variety of measurement strategies, such as rating scales, observations, and written appraisals (Braskamp, Brandenburg, and Ory, 1984). In monitoring student progress or institutional effectiveness—two distinct endeavors subsumed under the name of assessment in higher education—there are a multitude of pieces of information that can be used. The selection of information should be based on its intended use. If the well-being of the faculty and staff is to be considered in the assessment program, which data to collect, how to summarize and interpret the data, and the audiences of the data need to be considered with this use in mind.

Use Requires a Triple-A Perspective. Assessment is critical to institutional effectiveness. But assessment alone is insufficient. It must be conceived and implemented as a part of an ongoing process that I like to call "assessment, analysis, and action" (AAA). The third part is the key because its inclusion forces us to think about the end result—the outcome—of assessment. If we measure student outcomes, student activities during college, precollege characteristics, campus culture, faculty activities, or curriculum, we need to think in terms of how that information can be used to improve the effectiveness of the institution. The focus on analysis is equally important. If we focus too narrowly on student outcomes—that is, if we collect only information about student growth and not about student activities, curriculum, student life experiences, faculty, or culture—we will have difficulty analyzing and interpreting the data. If we wish to discuss possible reasons for student outcomes variability, we need to have information about the plausible influences.

Just as diagnosis without treatment is not very helpful to a sick patient, assessment without analysis and action can do little for an institution. No institution is entirely healthy, so improvement is always possible and maintenance of well-being is critical. For maximum use, assessment must measure potential influences on outcomes so that the faculty and staff who are responsible for students' learning and growth environments have enough information to be able to affect these influences, and thus better meet the goals for student growth and development.

References

Braskamp, L. A., Brandenburg, D. C., and Ory, J. C. *Evaluating Teaching Effectiveness: A Guidebook.* Newbury Park, Calif.: Sage, 1984.
Braskamp, L. A., and Krug, S. *High Investment Organizations: A Source Book.* Champaign, Ill.: MetriTech, 1989.
Cross, K. P. "Feedback in the Classroom: Making Assessment Matter." Paper presented at the assessment forum of the American Association of Higher Education, Chicago, June 1988.
Hackman, J. R. "The Psychology of Self Management in Organizations." In M. S. Pallack and R. O. Perloff (eds.), *Psychology and Work: Productivity, Change and Employment.* Washington, D.C.: American Psychological Association, 1986.
Lawler, E. E., III. *High-Involvement Management: Participative Strategies for Improving Organizational Performance.* San Francisco: Jossey-Bass, 1986.
Maehr, L. M., and Braskamp, L. A. *The Motivation Factor: A Theory of Personal Investment.* Lexington, Mass.: Lexington Books, 1986.
Mento, A. J., Steele, R. P., and Karren, R. J. "A Meta-Analytic Study of the Effects of Goal Setting on Task Performance: 1966-1984." *Organizational Behavior and Human Decision Processes,* 1987, *39,* 52-83.
Schön, D. A. *The Reflective Practitioner.* New York: Basic Books, 1983.
Wildavsky, A. "The Self-Evaluating Organization." *Public Administration Review,* 1972, *32* (5), 509-520.

Larry A. Braskamp is acting dean of the College of Applied Life Sciences at the University of Illinois, Urbana-Champaign.

Assessment focuses attention on the identification of incongruities or dysfunctionalities in academic programming. Analyses of the data must involve specific user groups with interests in the programs.

Assessment and Academic Judgments in Higher Education

George M. Dennison, Mary Anne Bunda

Assessment programs in higher education ought to provoke good internal evaluation efforts. Nonetheless, the current literature makes it difficult to define assessment as an effective evaluation program. Evaluation typically entails the systematic collection and analysis of information that people care about so as to answer unique questions about a program. Specific evaluation projects are rarely longitudinal in nature. Using information as evidence to answer real questions raised by actual users characterizes evaluation, whereas identifying and producing useful outcomes information results from assessment. An array of different audiences and clients for assessment information presents very significant problems requiring careful thought and planning in order to ensure evaluation as the ultimate outcome.

As discussed in the higher education literature, assessment differs significantly from evaluation. One might best characterize assessment as a method or group of methods designed to accumulate information perhaps useful as evidence in evaluation—that is, assessment is a prelude to evaluation and a necessary one. As a result, much of the literature on assessment concentrates on defending the concept of measurement itself

(Ewell, 1985b) or on techniques of measurement (Ewell, 1985a), rather than on the uses of information. In a disconcerting way, the objects and objectives of assessment shift radically, in accordance with the information needs of the users, from a focus on the individual student (as in the use of a rising junior examination) (Adelman, 1984), to an institutional program (such as general education), to a program of a specific department (such as majors assessment), to a vague concept of institutional accountability (such as the requirement for institutional effectiveness data imposed by some accrediting agency), or to a special purpose involving a single methodology or a single instrument (such as an alumni survey or the use of the Graduate Record Examination). Some of the literature attempts to link the assessment process to program review efforts (Ewell, 1983) but usually with few specifics.

The seemingly endless array of uses and purposes tends to confuse discussions of assessment, and the advocates of differing approaches rarely explain how the resultant information contributes to the overall evaluation effort. The internal institutional focus of assessment for curriculum evaluation and revision has rarely been addressed. As a result, the critics of assessment have had a field day exposing the apparent contradictions and potential dangers. Because they have neglected consideration of use and focus, the proponents of assessment as a means of producing relevant information have not responded well to charges of imprudent waste of scarce institutional resources or to playing into the hand of external groups and agencies by offering up information that typically does more harm than good when it focuses attention on irrelevant or meaningless but dangerous and simplistic comparisons.

Any institutional benefits of assessment will result directly from the clarity and comprehensiveness of its definition and methodology. To rely on the administration of a single instrument to set priorities or establish budgets will not improve the decision-making process of any institution. To accept surveys of attitudes as the essential consideration in evaluating the effectiveness of a program hardly enhances the credibility of the decisions rendered. The issue here relates both to how the institution collects information, because we surely need valid, reliable, and relevant information, and to the uses of information. To that extent, assessment resembles evaluation, but only in terms of methodology. In the most functional relation, assessment serves evaluation by providing portions—the important portions that relate to student outcomes—of the necessary information base.

Clearly, some assessment efforts speak to this relationship more directly than others, but all actually have that function. Of the uses already mentioned, three serve evaluation indirectly while two do so directly. Any assessment effort relying on the administration of a single instrument reveals something about the current practices or concerns of the institution—as, for example, a preoccupation with the effectiveness of the general education program or with outcomes in the major—but will not ensure a comprehensive evaluation because of the effort's limited scope and coverage. Just so, well-designed alumni surveys offer a general sense of the perceptions of graduates and how they change over time, but the information requires careful analysis for use in an evaluation. Rising junior examinations with their focus on progress beyond certain skill levels may or may not reveal much about the quality of the curriculum, since they typically encourage teaching to the test. In the K-12 sector, statewide testing has all too frequently produced so-called curricular reforms reducing educational programming to the "basics" while ignoring higher-level development in students. Assessment used to ensure accountability—whether by accrediting agencies, coordinating commissions, governors, or state legislatures—usually produces such vague results that the external regulators can justify any action they please. And such assessment systems usually cost as much or more than comprehensive systems that serve internal decision making (Ewell and Jones, 1985).

Nonetheless, these uses of assessment can serve as the beginning of structured inquiry about the institution, if the assessment is properly conceived, administered, and analyzed. In other words, assessment results represent the starting point, not the end. As examples, the assessment (that is, the measurements) of the effectiveness of the general education program or of outcomes in the major fields of study may relate directly to the purposes of an evaluation and therefore appear easier to justify and to support. No one questions the need to evaluate the success of the general education program in developing the desired skills and understanding, although disagreement rages as to whether one can ever assess (measure) the outcomes with sufficient rigor to defend the results (Bok, 1986). Many people argue the same with regard to outcomes in the major. To these critics, education involves such complex and multifaceted components that attempts to measure the outcomes accomplish nothing more than trivializing important considerations. These critics generally concede that assessment as practiced at Alverno College—a process of ongoing evaluation of skills and competencies of students by experts in the field, with an accompanying requirement of mastery prior to advancement—responds to their concerns, but such an approach exceeds the capacity of institutions with large enrollments (Mentkowski and Loacker, 1985). To compound the problem, a large school typically involves a federation of colleges or schools, and each of the federated units is responsible for part of the institutional environment and for providing a distinct portion of the education. Admitting some overlap or duplication, the units usually pursue their own goals and objectives and assume that institutional coherence will result. Within this context, to federate fully the assessment and evaluative functions abandons the critical concern for the development among graduates of the skills, knowledge, and attitudes presumably common to all educated people.

How, then, does an institution committed to assessment as a means to focus attention on the curriculum and the learning environment accomplish its purpose? In recent months, the spate of articles and special conferences dealing with the nitty-gritty, how-to concerns of assessment have provided no little advice and counsel. Those interested have several examples for guidance from colleges and universities as different in role and mission as Alverno College, Northeast Missouri State University, George Mason University, University of Tennessee at Knoxville, and Clayton State College. In what follows, we will focus on this concern for an effective approach and offer some general as well as specific suggestions that reflect our experience in the effort to develop and implement a successful assessment program.

It bears remarking that we approach assessment as an internal institutional function, perhaps mandated but certainly not controlled externally. In our view, the most appropriate role for assessment relates it to an ongoing evaluation effort intended to help restore coherence to baccalaureate education (Halpern, 1987). We doubt the efficacy of assessment defined as a means to ensure accountability, for it seems clear to us that other means to this end have greater potential. More important, we remain persuaded that the diversion of assessment resources to serve external accountability purposes will destroy its inherent usefulness for institutional revitalization.

Assessment Within the Institution

The administrator who initiates assessment within an institution has a role and responsibility quite distinct from that of the person who conducts the assessment studies. In addition, those using the assessment results at the program level have interests and concerns that diverge from those of the initiator and conductor. However, all three share a common obligation to clarify the objects and objectives of the effort and to identify the relevant uses according to the needs of the several audiences and client groups.

These relationships deserve careful analysis and delineation at the outset.

The initiating administrator has an obvious interest in obtaining useful and usable information. In most cases, the initiating administrator wants longitudinal and norm-referenced information, allowing internal and external comparisons. In addition, the initiator needs to explain clearly how and why the information serves needs from a variety of different perspectives. On the other hand, the conductor of the assessments must maintain a neutral posture designed to assure all users of the security and reliability of the data obtained. Finally, the user groups have the responsibility to interpret the data within a meaningful context that relates to the programs involved. The program users tend to view each round of assessment studies as unique opportunities for internal program evaluation. These distinctive and quite different roles and responsibilities necessitate thoughtful attention to the function and purpose of assessment.

The conductor of assessment has the critical responsibility to guarantee to all users the relevance, reliability, and security of the data. Without the resultant sense of trust, assessment will not serve the purposes of evaluation, judgment, and curricular reform or revision, but will lead instead into interminable arguments about the significance and/or validity of the questions asked and data generated. Thus, from our perspective, the person charged to conduct assessment studies becomes a quasi-independent information broker who releases the information only to those with the right to know. Even the appearance of departure from this posture will undermine the acceptance and credibility of the studies conducted.

Once assessment results exist, the colleges and departments use them in self-evaluations that lead to conclusions regarding curricular or environmental change that will resolve problems. Evaluations conducted by the colleges or departments, of course, contain process information concerning the nature of the programs and judgments about the acceptability of the outcomes identified by the assessment studies. In this way, assessment serves evaluation at the program level and supports necessary change. Quite clearly, the users have greater confidence in the information because of the posture of the assessment conductor, and concomitantly the evaluation has a greater chance of having a solid information base to serve as evidence, as a direct result.

Use of assessment results at the program level, however, does not exhaust their functionality. The university governance structure also relies on the assessment studies to provide an informed context for analysis, evaluation, and judgment. Certainly, the faculty committees use information differently than administrators, but all need it. The administrator who initiates assessment must include the results in program and budget planning to give credibility to the effort. Failure to do so will undermine any assessment effort. Thus, assessment not only serves but virtually requires institutional as well as program evaluation by virtue of the need to pay attention to assessment results.

The definition of the objects and objectives of assessment seems simple at first glance, but it requires great care. We must all by now realize the dangers and difficulties involved in the seemingly reasonable and straightforward task of setting priorities as to desired student outcomes. To initiate an assessment effort relative to these priorities, those responsible must identify the audiences that have legitimate stakes in the results of assessment and must determine the appropriate amount of influence each audience should have over the design of the assessment. In the process, those responsible will undoubtedly find it necessary to dispel the common misconception that assessment means the use of a single instrument or a single administration of several instruments to generate data useful in curricular and environmental decisions. In order to succeed, assessment studies must focus at once so sharply that the results have immediate application to program redesign and so broadly that the data elements will not change significantly over an extended period. At the same time, the results obtained must satisfy the needs of (1) those directly responsible for the object of the assessment, (2) those who serve in an advisory or policy-making capacity, (3) those who provide support services, and (4) those generally responsible for institutional operations. And it helps to have the ability to walk on water, even though demonstrating that capability elicits a corresponding charge that one cannot swim.

Of course, it defies logic and reason to attempt to put into place all these elements and serve all these uses simultaneously. Much, it seems to us, depends on how a particular institution organizes its programs and the complexity of the governance system within the institution. Thus, any institution contemplating assessment must impose its own imprimatur on the process. Structures and strategies that lead to appropriate use of the assessment results must reflect the context within which the assessment occurs. Institutions seeking to pull from the shelf and implement a ready-made assessment process will do so at their own peril.

Assessment at Western Michigan University

In order to explain the assessment process at Western Michigan University (WMU), we must begin with a brief description of the institutional setting. The WMU faculty takes great pride in the institutional designation as the only doctoral I university in the state, granting at least forty Ph.D.'s annually in five or more academic programs, and one of five "graduate-intensive" institutions. The state of Michigan does not have a coordinating board or commission but accords constitutional autonomy to each of the fifteen publicly supported universities. The institutions themselves vary tremendously in terms of role and mission, program mix, size, and complexity. Therefore, it seems highly unlikely that the state of Michigan will ever adopt legislation such as the Florida rising junior examination or the Tennessee incentive appropriations approach. Rather, it seems most likely that assessment in Michigan will serve institutional purposes.

The university has six academic colleges that offer undergraduate majors, one college that provides course work for all majors in the "general" and "integrative studies" mode, an honors college, and a graduate college. The on-campus enrollment for fall semester 1988 reached roughly 22,000, with an additional 3,000 students registered through five regional centers located around the state. Graduate students, including those off campus, account for 25 percent of the total student population, the third highest ratio in the state, and the university has attained the second highest ratio of off- to on-campus enrollments.

The only comprehensive university in the western part of the state, WMU aspires to fulfill a mandate to promote economic development and cultural enrichment of the surrounding region. As a result, the research agenda of the faculty tends to reflect the identified needs of external groups, while also responding to the initiatives of state and national agencies. The mission statement that has captured the imagination of the faculty defines WMU as a regional institution with state and national responsibilities in instruction, research, and service.

The governance structure of the university places heavy emphasis on participation and shared responsibilities. The faculty senate includes administrators as ex officio and full voting members along with elected faculty members. The senate conducts most of its delegated and advisory functions through a complex array of councils and committees, with final approval of curricular and other policy changes by the president. The board of trustees reserves to itself consideration of all new degree programs and organizational changes involving the basic structure of the university. As a result, the university maintains a very comprehensive governance system that requires the active participation of the faculty and thus assumes rather substantial time commitments.

The Office of University Assessment, established last year as an entity within academic affairs under the direct oversight of the provost, cooperates with but remains independent of the Office of Institutional Research. This arrangement reflects the institutional posture that assessment will serve curricular ends. Table 1 presents a description of the various program components of the Office of University Assessment and the relations involved. The listing of the components and the rationale for each provides some measure of the complexity of the internal relations. The prescribed indicators clearly reflect a marriage of institutional and programmatic concerns.

The listing in Table 1 provides insight regarding the organizational arrangements at the university. Most important, we have chosen not to establish new and mission-oriented advisory committees and councils for the assessment effort. Instead, the assessment program components rely on the existing structures for counsel, advice, guidance, implementation, interpretation, and response, with some exceptions. We have taken this position based on the conviction that assessment information will prove useful to the extent that it fits within and meets the needs of the existing institutional structure. In our view, the alternative approach of erecting new structures leads directly into internal divisiveness because of the apparent threat to existing entities. In addition, we believe that the chosen organizational approach brings the assessment information to bear

Table 1. Assessment Methods and Client Analysis

Indicators and Clients	Entry Diagnosis	University Level — Intellectual Skills	University Level — General Education	Majors	Academic Support Programs	Campus Environment
Objective indicators	Entering ACT intellectual skills exam a. Reading b. Writing c. Math skill Fine art portfolio Placement exam a. Math b. Chemistry c. Foreign language CLEP tests	End-of-course exam CAAP (ACT) PPST (ETS)	COMP (ACT)	Majors device Certification exams GRE • GMAT LSAT • NTE MCAT • DAT Placements	User rates Retention impact Employment statistics	User rates
Subjective judgmental indicators	HSGPA Transcript analysis In-house survey	GPA IGI(ETS) ESS(ACT) In-house survey a. Leavers b. Current c. Alumni	GPA IGI(ETS) ESS(ACT)	GPA(overall) GPA(major) CSEQ(HERI) In-house survey a. Leavers b. Current c. Alumni	ESS(ACT) CSEQ(HERI) IGI(ETS) In-house survey a. Leavers b. Current c. Alumni	ESS(ACT) CSEQ(HERI) IGI(ETS) In-house survey a. Leavers b. Current c. Alumni
User groups	Provost Senate AFA&SSC Admissions office College curriculum committee and dean Department where applicable	Provost Senate USC Program unit	Provost Senate USC College curriculum committee and dean	Provost Department unit College in professional school case	Provost Senate USC, AFA&SSC Operating unit	Provost Senate USC, AFA&SSC Operating unit Other vice-presidents when appropriate

at the level closest to the actual delivery of programs; thus, it optimizes the possibilities for meaningful effect because the users participate actively in determining the significance of the information and help to give concrete form to its consequences.

Because of this approach, we have also built on existing functions within the university. The Undergraduate Studies Council of the faculty senate has great influence on the general curricular decisions of the university. The president and provost rarely reject its recommendations, respecting the tradition that the faculty should exercise profound influence over the curriculum. Through its deliberations, the council provides the several colleges and departments with definitions of the integral components of baccalaureate curricula offered within those colleges and departments, but departments are required to interpret the definitions within a disciplinary context. Thus, the council defines the general education program, at present a combination of specified skills (reading, writing, mathematics, and computing) and distribution requirements (arts and humanities, social sciences, natural sciences, and cross-cultural or non-Western studies). These definitions serve as the guidelines for program planning and development at the college and department levels, with review through the structure of college and university committees.

In order to ensure that function follows structure, assessment reports go to the college and department committees for analysis and action. To be sure, the university committees and councils also receive the reports, as do the chairs, deans, and provost. And, to some extent, these administrators or university councils and committees intervene in the curricular process to suggest or mandate particular attention to specific information about program effectiveness. But the college and department committees have the responsibility to make use of the reports, and they typically require additional information before completing their analyses and taking action. The data collected by the committees or councils speak to the specific evaluative questions within their realms of responsibility. The Office of University Assessment provides the information requested and protects the integrity of the process by withholding the reports from all except those with a need to know. In essence, the assessment reports serve the curricular planning process and not the desire to enhance the institutional image or the necessity to respond to external groups and agencies.

Assessment Studies in Progress

The Office of University Assessment has initiated several studies within the last year. To facilitate these efforts, the provost and the director discussed each extensively with the affected faculty organizations and groups. The purposes of each study received appropriate attention, and the faculty participated actively in the planning process. Quite clearly, the second imperative for a successful assessment program dictates the early involvement of the faculty in order to promote the sense of ownership without which the program cannot succeed. If the faculty believe in the assessment effort and accept it because of its potential to aid in curricular revision, they will persuade the students that it has legitimate purposes. Without active faculty and student involvement, no assessment can succeed. The university can mandate participation, but assessment requires active and meaningful participation, not mere formalities.

The WMU assessment effort has thrusts relating to placement of admitted students, general education, outcomes in the majors, and alumni satisfaction, among others. Most institutions currently have programs designed to assist in the appropriate placement of admitted students; not many, however, view this activity as an assessment function. We include it within assessment so as to coordinate periodic reviews of placement instruments and policies within the various curricula and to relate placement to external norms wherever and whenever possible. Assessment in the majors occurs within a set of policy guidelines (listed in Figure 1). Each department has developed a procedure that meets a particular set of concerns consistent with the purposes of assessment at WMU. In what follows, we will describe two thrusts at the institutional level as examples. In one case, the assessment project uses a nationally available standardized instrument relevant to an academic program across the institution, while the other case uses a locally developed instrument that addresses academic programs and student services functions. These studies exemplify our approach while using two distinct methodologies.

ACT-COMP. We designed a study of the general education program using the objective form of the ACT-COMP (American College Testing's College Outcomes Measurement Program) with random samples of freshmen and seniors to whom we have administered the instrument (Forrest and Steele, 1982). The freshman sample was a true representative sample, while the seniors were randomly asked to volunteer. The COMP matches the university's definition of general education adequately, as it covers social sciences, natural sciences, and humanities, and produces skill subscores that are of interest to the faculty. Additionally, we chose it because the individual students receive information concerning their development not available at the same cost of time and money with the Educational Testing Service instrument (Academic Profile).

We prepared materials for primary curriculum policy-making agencies that showed the fit between the objectives of the COMP and those of the general education program of the university. Additionally, we invited all faculty members who serve on curriculum committees at the college and university levels to participate in an administration of the COMP so that they would have some hands-on experience with the test. Faculty understanding of the instrument is essential to its acceptance. The acceptance of COMP as a good but partial indicator of the effectiveness of the

Figure 1. Majors Assessment Policies

The purpose of assessment is to provide information about the curriculum, not to make judgments about individual students. However, individual students should, if possible, receive useful information from assessment procedures. The assessment information provides the department with the opportunity to interact individually with graduating seniors. The thrust of the counsel provided by the faculty to the student is likely to focus on post graduation plans. The assessment system designed for the departments and the colleges must be consistent with the policy of the university as a whole.

1. All assessment devices must be reviewed for curricular validity by department faculty. The organizational structure for the review can vary across departments.
    a. Since the department curriculum committee is the major audience for any analysis of the majors assessment data, some departments have delegated the responsibility for the validity of assessment devices to the curriculum committees.
    b. The complexity of the outcomes within the major has led other departments to form a special review and design committee with expertise in the special skills expected in the major. This group, formed by the curriculum committee, generally is disbanded once the assessment device is in place. However, the members are likely to serve as in-house consultants to the department curriculum committee when reports of majors assessment are considered.
    c. In some departments, the members serve as a committee of the whole in the development of the assessment device. One faculty member generally serves as the assessment coordinator. He or she implements the plan and serves as the liaison with the Office of University Assessment.
2. Locally developed components of assessment will be reviewed by experts in the field.
    a. Norm-referenced devices provide departments with outside benchmarks of student achievement. The relevance of the information is judged by the validity of the instrument itself and the comparability of the norm group to the student population at Western Michigan University.
    b. Internally developed instruments and procedures lack the external benchmark of actual student performance and, hence, must rely on professional judgments. The department assessment coordinators (generally the curriculum committee) are responsible for the selection of the individual expert. The charge to the consultant is:
        (1) To verify that the table of specifications developed for the assessment devices matches the description of the major provided by the department
        (2) To verify that the draft device adequately meets the table of specifications
        (3) To verify that the description of the major is relevant to professional standards.
    c. The assessment device developed by the department need not be limited to a single instrument nor to a single methodology.
        (1) While a multiple-choice format provides efficient scoring procedures, other methodologies might be considered.

Figure 1. *(continued)*

  (2) The variety of outcomes in the major, as specified by the department, strongly influences the number and type of devices used.
  (3) Methods that require professional judgment in the evaluation of student responses, such as portfolio analysis or performance analysis, must be accompanied by clearly developed criteria to be used by the judges, specifications of selection procedures for the judges, and stipulations of the number of judges.
3. Assessment information will be collected with individual student identifiers so that data might be linked for analytical purposes to student academic records and other relevant demographic data.
4. No test scores will be used to deny academic credentials to a student, if that student has successfully completed coursework requirements.
 a. Scores from assessment generally are not entered in the student's master file.
 b. The Office of University Assessment maintains a separate student data base.
5. Assessment should provide a longitudinal data base that can be used for internal decision making. No single data point should be used, exclusively, to make major academic decisions.
 a. Changes in assessment map major changes in the curriculum.
 b. Emphasis in assessment is given to the most stable aspects of a major.
6. Assessment information is provided on a regular basis to individuals charged with the development and monitoring of academic programs.
 a. The Office of the University Assessment provides information concerning general universitywide curricular outcomes to college and university committees and councils.
 b. The Office of University Assessment provides majors assessment results to the department.
  (1) The department may use this information in accreditation reports.
  (2) The department may use this information as the basis for revision requests to college- and university-level committees.
  (3) The department may use this information as part of a rationale for additional personnel.
  (4) The department may use this information to trigger an evaluation of the program.
   (a) The Office of University Assessment will provide the department with consultation on the design and/or methodology.
   (b) A critical component of any evaluation is the collection of information on the learning experiences provided to the students.
   (c) Perceptual data may also be collected from both faculty members and students.
7. Administration of the assessment is scheduled and performed by the department.
 a. Publicly available instruments are ordered institutionally by the Office of University Assessment.
 b. Locally developed instruments are processed on campus. Consultation in scoring and analysis are provided by the Office of University Assessment.

general education program was essential to the success of the assessment program. Unless faculty are willing appreciate the imperfect match between any instrument and a given program, they will not see the need for multiple measures. Assessment discussions under those conditions degenerate into an endless search for the perfect instrument. We sought to avoid that result, not only because the search for one instrument reinforces the belief that assessment means using a single indicator but also because we recognize the imperfections of all instruments. Faculty reviews of complex curricular matters require equally complex data sets.

Because the COMP is norm-referenced, it provides external benchmarks. This is particularly important at our institution because the faculty admit to no peer school within the state. Moreover, our first analytical questions had very little to do with the high-anxiety issues of differences among our own colleges. A university report was prepared for the faculty senate and for the Undergraduate Studies Council. Deans and chairs of college curriculum committees received the university report and supplements describing their own colleges. Because of the large number of graduates who transfer from other postsecondary institutions, we were concerned about differences between beginners and transfer students. In all likelihood, this specific use of the instrument marks a substantial difference from the use common at smaller institutions with a focus sharply on "native" students.

Most faculty members accept this approach as a means to establish a data base to analyze some of the assumptions used to design degree and general education requirements, but more data are clearly needed. The concern for data has initiated a change in policy. The size of the senior volunteer sample was so small that a graduate requirement for participation in assessment has been put into place for 1989-90. Assessment in general education has now been institutionalized. We have announced the new requirement to students and opened the option of 1988-89 senior participation. We persuaded the students of the unfairness of withholding the individual assessment option from the 1988-89 graduates. This characterization of assessment at WMU as an information service to all constituents has led to almost complete but fully voluntary participation by 1988-89 graduates. It seems clear that we have managed to begin the transition toward the institutionalization of assessment as a common value.

Moreover, the analysis of the freshman prompted concern about student skills in using both verbal and quantitative symbols. This area of concern provides a focus for conversations with high schools about needed skills development. At the same time, the results of the program have allowed us to design new data collection efforts that provide more precise information about the levels of skill in the use of symbols. To this end, WMU has become a lead institution in ACT's Collegiate Assessment of Academic Proficiency program, relying on the Critical Thinking module as a measure of critical reading—that is, of using verbal symbols effectively.

Alumni Survey. We have just completed a survey of two graduating cohorts (1981 and 1986) to assess the perceptions of the alumni with respect to the quality of their experience and to measure the frequency of some behaviors we consider indicative of a university education. The satisfaction of alumni with the institutional environment and the academic programs is of concern to a wide number of audiences within the institution—academic affairs, student affairs, and alumni affairs. Thus, this endeavor moved outside the academic governance structure, requiring the establishment of new advisory panels. Using two classes provided some measure of change in perception. Additionally, we developed the survey instrument by asking each of the chairs, deans, and student services directors about the information they needed regarding alumni satisfaction. During this process, we discovered a great deal of predictable variation among the units with respect to contact with the alumni. We have shared the results of the alumni survey with all appropriate units within the institution. As a result, we have universal support for this study.

Because the alumni information base was relevant to individuals in nonacademic units that fall outside of the collegiate and faculty senate governance structures, we had to create two separate internal review panels during the development process to assure involvement of the client groups. A prime user panel at the institutional level consisted of a representative from alumni relations, student services, and academic affairs. This panel considered the study design from the perspective of the usefulness of the information for the development and revision of programs. A technical review panel, composed of experts in survey methodology, reviewed the instrument and cover letter for technical adequacy prior to mailing. The members of the latter panel represented the array of constituencies involved and served not only as a valuable resource in the development process but also lent credibility to the whole study.

While the alumni data relate to a very different perspective on outcomes of college in comparison to the COMP data, the proposed use of the information for program and policy review reflects the general assessment objectives. Therefore, in addition to college reports for the curriculum committees, we provided each dean and student services director with a report for the professional advisement staff or other nonacademic staff within the unit or college. As a result, the use by the college committees enhances the coordination of change efforts within the university by bringing together academic and student affairs personnel. After discussing the results of the alumni report, the Admissions, Financial Aid, and Student Services Council requested more information on current use of the recreational facilities on campus in order to explore the differential use by students revealed by the alumni data.

Administrative Uses of Assessment

All too frequently assessment programs become entangled with administrative issues of planning and budgeting. And why not? The information provided by a sound assessment program certainly should influence planning and budgeting on any campus. Otherwise we would have to assume that administrators act without regard for information, reflecting their biases and the private deals negotiated behind closed doors. That may be a good description of reality in some situations but, we hope, not all. Nonetheless, we urge careful attention to the obvious concerns of faculty members about the potential uses of information available through assessment programs.

At Western Michigan University, we define the primary function of assessment as facilitation of the improvement of the academic programs and the educational environment. Thus, those administrators who use assessment information to encourage faculty responsiveness to identified areas of concern receive recognition for their efforts. In addition, those who identify problems after careful analysis of assessment information and propose needed changes that require additional resources have received assurances of responsive action, within the constraints of available resources.

To ensure appropriate administrative use of assessment data, we involved the deans and chairs at the outset. With the purposes of assessment clearly articulated, the academic administrators participated actively in the design of each assessment study and the use of its results. The president's and the provost's support for the program provided a clear indication of the priority that assessment has within the university. Experience to date indicates that academic administrators have accepted assessment on those terms.

Of course, it remains to be seen what the impact of assessment, as a whole, will be. On the other hand, the institution has already benefited. The commitment of the university to assessment as the means to enhance the quality of the student learning experience has gained attention across the state. High school students, parents, and counselors know of the effort and comment favorably about it. In addition, the alumni survey revealed favorable attitudes in general about the institution and its programs. While the assessment effort focuses on internal purposes, the reports nonetheless provide incidental benefits, even if they sometimes contain critical comments. As the major consideration, we deliberately sought to convince the public at large of the determination of the university to conduct such studies and to use the reports to improve the programs and environment for future generations of students.

Premises of Practice

We have not engaged in assessment nearly as long at Western Michigan University as some have at other institutions, and authors of other chapters in this sourcebook certainly have much more experience than we do. Therefore, we confess to some discomfort when telling other people how to do it. But we have started the process at the university, and we believe that we have learned some lessons or confirmed some premises that may help others similarly situated. In that spirit, we offer just three premises of good practice in assessment.

First, make very clear the objects and objectives of the assessment program. In our view, assessment reflects an institutional commitment of service to students. The institution must make clear that student development ranks as the highest priority. Rhetorical flourishes certainly help, but rhetoric must reflect reality to have credibility. If everyone in the institution understands this ultimate objective, then resistance dissipates and artificial barriers preventing cooperation among student affairs personnel, academic administrators, and faculty come down without much additional effort. The level of such cooperation for the alumni survey conducted at Western Michigan University corroborates this essential premise.

The purposes of the assessment program must be clearly and directly related to curricular and environmental change for the purpose of promoting student learning. If assessment has even the suspected purpose of evaluating faculty performance, its acceptance will suffer accordingly and appropriately so. The assessment of student outcomes involves such complex issues as to render the results useless for an individual faculty member's evaluation. Even to suggest that use will subvert the entire effort.

In addition, we believe clarity of purpose requires a straightforward statement that the results of student outcomes assessment will not determine whether a student graduates or not. In our view, to premise graduation on the results of a single exit examination penalizes the student for the failure of the institution. If students fulfill course and other requirements for graduation, performance in an assessment activity—except where an institution has a program similar to that at Alverno College—should not affect graduation. We believe, however, that students should receive the results of their performance in assessment activities because of the potential to assist them in future planning. We have found that students value these results and participate voluntarily and sincerely in the assessment program in exchange for the confidential results.

The second premise of assessment requires the involvement of the faculty from the outset, thereby securing their commitment to use the results in decision making. If the administrators responsible for the assessment program make very clear their willingness not only to consult with but also to heed the counsel provided by faculty, then a sense of collaboration and program ownership results. The faculty will not participate if they sense a move to undermine their prerogatives as curriculum designers and developers. Nor will they accord much credence to a program that unabashedly purports to justify budget decisions. While the assessment results can and will influence program and budget decisions over time, the faculty must have a sense that the initial purpose relates directly to program improvement.

Thus, assessment reports must not tell faculty members what to conclude about the program or which revisions to institute. In a very subtle way, assessment reports must point to areas of concern, suggesting the need for sustained analysis by those responsible for the program in order to determine how to respond to possible weaknesses or failure to accomplish intended results. Therefore, if the assessment reports become the bases for budget decisions without additional analysis, they lose their greatest potential to bring about improvement.

To reiterate, assessment efforts require the involvement of all segments of the faculty, new as well as old and senior as well as junior, in an environment designed to foster dialogue about the teaching and learning process and its intended outcomes. Unless faculty have a sense of ownership, the process become threatening rather than empowering. Of course, assessment in and of itself cannot guarantee empowerment. But it can and will, if properly implemented, provide the occasion for meaningful participation.

The third assessment premise mandates that those responsible must explain the differences between the process they envision and distinct but related evaluative efforts—namely, program review and program evaluation. Most faculty members have had a great deal of experience with evaluation, whether of individual performances or of program effectiveness. In addition, most faculty members tend to identify program review as a prelude to program and budget cutting or reduction within the institution. Assessment provides information useful and valuable in evaluation and program review efforts, but it does not constitute program evaluation or review in and of itself. Instead, assessment stands on its own to ensure relevant and reliable information to faculty members interested in the quality and responsiveness of the programs they have developed. Defined in this way and carefully differentiated from evaluation and program review, assessment has a very positive thrust and typically elicits an enthusiastic response from faculty.

These three premises of successful practice will, we believe, produce incidental benefits to the institution as well. The longitudinal data base provided through well-designed assessment efforts not only empower and enable faculty members to conduct thorough and informed self-studies of the programs they maintain but also offer a context for meaningful comparative analysis and judgment by responsible administrators. The assessment conductor ensures the provision of usable and reliable data; the faculty responsible for the program provide a context for interpreting the data; and, as a result, the academic administrators have a rational and comparative foundation for judgments about quality, effectiveness, and responsiveness. In the end, the students reap the major benefits from these synergistic and symbiotic relationships that focus attention on the provision of a coherent academic experience.

The three premises of successful practice in assessment and their consequences in responsible academic programming work to guard against inappropriate comparisons that result from the misuse of the data. Faculty view with alarm any comparisons that do not result from the application of carefully drawn criteria and reasonable bases. Assessment and evaluation work well only with prior agreement about the appropriateness of subsequent comparisons for the purpose of illuminating judgments about quality, effectiveness, and responsiveness. Typically, faculty members accept comparisons to peer programs or institutions if they are satisfied with the definition of a peer. To draw invidious comparisons among and between colleges within a university hardly meets that requirement. And making comparisons of that kind will very quickly deprive an assessment program of its potential benefits.

On the other hand, soundly based and well-articulated comparisons usually overcome faculty concerns about the uses of the information derived from assessment. Those responsible for the quality and effectiveness of the programs will attend to the results of reasonable comparisons, if given the opportunity to assist in the definition and interpretation of the data concerning those programs. Many administrators have commented that faculty serve as the best and sharpest critics of academic programs if empowered and enabled to participate in meaningful evaluations. Assessment provides the foundation for that outcome.

In the assessment effort at Western Michigan University, we have agreed from the outset that we will use national norms only from comparable institutions in order to determine how well we have succeeded in the accomplishment of our stated goals. Thus, we have emphasized the gains students register in a value-added sense compared to students enrolled at peer institutions. In addition, we have used assessment information to inform ourselves generally about the performance of students from high schools with college preparation programs as compared to the performance of those who did not have the benefit of such programs. In a similar way, we have compared the success of transfer students with that of "native" students in order to learn more about the quality of the general education program offered at other institutions and at this university. Because as many as half of the graduates each year originally transferred from other institutions rather than beginning as freshmen, we have a great and abiding interest in determining how we can best meet their needs.

Conclusion

The topic of assessment has stirred considerable discussion and controversy across the country during recent years. Touted variously as a useful way to focus campus attention on student growth and development, to ensure accountability, to make certain that students acquire intended skills and knowledge before advancing or graduating, to measure institutional effectiveness, or any combination of these, assessment often appears to be a panacea. We identify with the first purpose in a belief that a well-conceived assessment program will provide information that helps to focus the ongoing effort to maintain academic programs and a campus environment of high quality in response to student needs and institutional purposes.

Moreover, we want to make clear our rejection of the view that mere testing constitutes good assessment. We subscribe to the use of reliable instruments that produce useful information about programs and institutions. But assessment involves much more. Most significant in terms of functionality, it requires the transformation of information into evidence that counts in the effort to identify areas for improvement and to analyze the consequences of such revisions. As such, the process of assessment leads to and helps to support academic judgments but does not determine them.

Thus, we conclude as we began. Assessment ought to provoke good internal evaluation efforts because of the relevant and reliable information it provides. But to stop with the acquisition of the information and to expect it to speak for itself augurs the failure of assessment. We believe that assessment has the best possible chance of success, and thereby fostering institutional revitalization, when those responsible for the delivery of educational programs participate actively in the design of the assessment, take ownership of the interpretation of the resulting information, and use the results as the basis for change to enhance student growth and development.

References

Adelman, C. *Starting with Students: Promising Approaches in American Higher Education.* Washington, D.C.: U.S. Government Printing Office, 1984.

Bok, D. C. *Higher Learning.* Cambridge, Mass.: Harvard University Press, 1986.

Ewell, P. T. *Program Reviews, Inputs and Outputs.* NCHEMS Monograph, no. 5. Boulder, Colo.: National Center for Higher Education Management Systems, 1983.

Ewell, P. T. (ed.). *Assessing Educational Outcomes.* New Directions for Institutional Research, no. 47. San Francisco: Jossey-Bass, 1985a.

Ewell, P. T. *Transformation Leadership for Improving Student Outcomes.* NCHEMS Monograph, no. 6. Boulder, Colo.: National Center for Higher Education Management Systems, 1985b.

Ewell, P. T., and Jones, D. P. *The Costs of Assessment.* NCHEMS Monograph, no. 8. Boulder, Colo.: National Center for Higher Education Management Systems, 1985.

Forrest, A., and Steele, J. *Defining and Measuring General Education Knowledge and Skills.* Iowa City, Iowa: American College Testing Program, 1982.

Halpern, D. F. (ed.). *Student Outcomes Assessment: What Institutions Stand to Gain.* New Directions for Higher Education, no. 59. San Francisco: Jossey-Bass, 1987.

Mentkowski, M., and Loacker, G. "Assessing and Validating the Outcomes of College." In P. T. Ewell (ed.), *Assessing Educational Outcomes.* New Directions for Institutional Research, no. 47. San Francisco: Jossey-Bass, 1985.

George M. Dennison is provost and vice-president for academic affairs and professor of history at Western Michigan University.

Mary Anne Bunda is director of the Office of University Assessment and professor of educational leadership at Western Michigan University.

In institutions of higher education, assessment finds its way into many areas of policy implementation.

A Role for Assessment in Higher Education Decision Making

John C. Ory

In Chapter Four, Dennison and Bunda define assessment as the collection and accumulation of information. The method for collecting and the type of information collected depend on the larger context of the study that requires the information. Whether the information is used for course, curriculum, or program evaluation or for personnel review or policy analysis, assessment serves these different processes by providing the necessary information.

Over the years, the Office of Instructional and Management Services (IMS) at the University of Illinois, Urbana–Champaign (UIUC) has been involved in the development and administration of several evaluation programs that contain an assessment component. Each of these programs addresses a campus need for information and provides useful information for campus decision makers.

The purpose of this chapter is to describe briefly UIUC evaluation programs in order to illustrate the many needs for and uses made of assessment information in a higher education setting. Considerations that were important in the development of each program are presented; then the programs themselves are described. Finally, we look at the campus needs met by and the uses made of each program.

Considerations for Program Development

IMS takes into account several considerations in the development and implementation of each evaluation program and its assessment component (Brandenburg, Braskamp, and Ory, 1979; Braskamp, Brandenburg, and Ory, 1984). Of major importance are the credibility, organizational fit, utility, and flexibility of each program.

Credibility. An evaluation program must have credibility with the involved audiences. Credibility must be earned over time through the successful implementation of programs with individual faculty, administrators, and students. It can only be gained if those implementing each program remain impartial, respect the prerogatives of individuals, and protect the confidentiality of the data collected. Credibility is also based on the perceptions of the audiences that the assessment information was appropriately selected, properly collected, and of adequate psychometric and technical quality.

In particular, this last component means that the assessment information is reliable, valid, and free from bias. For example, student ratings of instruction need to account for potential biases due to student, course, and instructor characteristics not considered to be indicative of instructor competence—for example, class size, required or elective nature of the course, grade earned in the course. The level of technical quality required can vary depending on the use made of the information; reliability must be higher for personnel-type decisions, for example, than for program improvement decisions. To strengthen audience and evaluator confidence in the quality of information, all parties should agree on minimally acceptable standards for instrument development, data collection procedures, and interpretation of data.

Organizational Fit. An evaluation program and its assessment component must fit into the governance and organizational structure of the institution. A productive program will complement, not usurp or divert, the existing organization and the flow of decision making within an institution. This entails getting the various audiences involved in the evaluation and assessment process and encouraging them to identify their needs and suggestions for change.

It also means that we, as evaluators, must remember that we provide information to decision makers so that they can make better programmatic, personnel, or policy decisions. Evaluators are seldom decision makers. Stated differently, we should follow Popham's (1975) third commandment for educational evaluators: "Honor thy decision maker: have no false decision makers before thee."

Utility. Our programs are designed and implemented to enhance the utilization of our findings. We try to provide information to users that is understandable, concise, and timely. Results may be rendered uninterpretable by lack of clarity, use of ambiguous terminology, or an overreliance on statistical information. A report that is not easily understood by a user can be interpreted in a number of ways, thus leading to confusion and risk to the credibility of the individual providing the information.

Conciseness and brevity are highly regarded by our university audience, especially administrators. One administrator has told us, "I want to see the report in one page. If it cannot be put on one page, then it is not worth commenting on." Many situations require us to analyze and interpret large amounts of data very quickly for the information to be most useful. Our audiences need information when they have to make decisions, not afterward. Therefore, it is critical to negotiate practical timelines and adhere to them to the extent possible.

Flexibility. We follow a multiple-purpose, criteria, source, method approach in the development of our programs. We recognize that identical information can be used for different purposes. For example, student ratings of instruction can be used for faculty improvement, for pay and rank decision making, and for student selection of courses. To accommodate all three purposes, we have included different types of items on student surveys and developed different reporting formats.

In the design of our programs, we recognize that there can be different criteria for judging quality. Two common dimensions of criteria are incorporated in most of our programs. The first dimension distinguishes between judging a program, project, or individual on the basis of input, process, or product. For example, do we judge instructional quality based on teacher behavior (process) or on the achievement of the students (product)? The second dimension distinguishes between implicit or explicit criteria. While explicit criteria are directly observable (test scores, for example), implicit criteria, such as colleague judgments, are more qualitative in nature.

We also recognize that different audiences use different criteria in making judgments of value, worth, and effectiveness. For example, departments differ in their criteria for effective teaching; some disciplines require laboratory or studio teaching while others do not. Therefore, we developed our student rating system to accommodate departmental cores or subsets of items that all faculty in a department must include on their evaluation questionnaires. Information is then provided that compares the ratings of all faculty teaching within a department.

Assessment information can be collected from many different sources through a variety of collection methods. Different sources and methods bring unique perspectives to an evaluation, thus allowing for the corroboration and verification of findings. For example, some individuals express themselves better orally than in writing. Our evaluation of the campus's freshman honors program combined student interviews with responses to written questionnaires. In another case, our system for administrator evaluations collects faculty responses to open-ended questions, to forced-choice items, and to interviews.

In sum, our office receives many requests to conduct evaluations and/or collect assessment information for different purposes from different audiences using different criteria and requiring different methods and different sources for data collection. Therefore, to satisfy this diversity of need and to provide fair and credible assessments, we follow a multiple-purpose, criteria, source, method approach in the development of our programs.

UIUC Evaluation Programs

Figure 1 shows the major UIUC evaluation programs and assessment components and indicates the campus needs addressed by each program, the uses made of assessment information, and the sources of and methods used for collecting information. A brief description of these programs follows.

Council on Program Evaluation (COPE). COPE represents a faculty-based system of evaluation intended to enhance quality in academic units. The evaluation of an academic program takes place every five to eight years. The COPE process was designed to avoid uniform campuswide prescriptive measures of quality and instead to rely primarily on the criteria and standards of excellence inherent in each discipline as the basis of judgment.

The following information is collected:
- Student major perceptions of programmatic aspects of unit
- Faculty evaluations of the performance of the unit head or chair and their perceptions of morale factors, unit operations procedures, and the effects of decisions made by administrators outside of the unit on the unit
- Departmental responses to a set of COPE questions (such as view of the discipline nationally, methods of handling curriculum problems)
- Data concerning tenure, promotion, courses taught, and budget.

Process. The vice-chancellor for academic affairs appoints a COPE council with nine faculty members (including five without administrative appointment), two undergraduate students, and two graduate students. Each year the council requests several units (selected on a cyclical basis) to conduct a self-evaluation in which the information just described is collected and summarized in a written report. Later, a public action report containing a summary of the self-evaluation, the recommendations made by the council, and the reaction of the unit to those recommendations is released.

Figure 1. Campus Assessment Efforts

	Administrator Evaluation	AP Program	COPE	Honors Evaluation	ICES	ITA Assessment	Math Statewide Testing	P&P System	Transition Evaluation
NEED FOR INFORMATION ABOUT:									
Administrator effectiveness	X								
Departmental quality		X							
Special or new program success			X	X		X			
Student course placement		X		X			X	X	X
Teaching effectiveness				X	X	X			X
DECISION MAKING USES:									
Course offerings		X	X	X		X	X	X	X
Course selection		X		X	X	X	X	X	X
Curriculum development		X	X	X	X		X	X	X
Faculty assignments				X	X	X	X		X
Personnel decisions (rank and pay)	X				X	X			
Program/Dept. modifications			X	X	X	X			X
Program/Dept. support decisions			X	X					
Recruitment of special populations		X			X		X	X	X
SOURCES OF INFORMATION:									
Administrators	X		X			X			
Alumni			X						
Content/discipline experts			X			X	X		
Documents and records	X	X	X	X		X	X	X	X
External audiences	X		X			X	X		
Faculty	X		X	X		X			X
Graduate students	X		X		X	X			
Potential undergraduate students		X		X			X	X	X
Staff	X			X		X			X
Undergraduate students	X			X	X	X		X	X
METHODS OF DATA COLLECTION:									
Document and record review	X	X	X	X		X	X	X	X
Examinations		X				X	X	X	X
Fixed-response survey items	X		X	X	X	X	X		X
Interviews	X		X	X		X	X		X
Open-ended survey items	X		X	X	X	X	X		X

Impact and Use. COPE was established in 1974 in response to a faculty/administration committee report stating that "we need on this campus new and better mechanisms and renewed dedication to enhance quality and to use available resources more wisely." Since 1974 all academic units have been "COPEd" at least twice. What has been the impact on campus?

The COPE process has produced both obvious and not so obvious outcomes. There have been many obvious changes attributed to COPE recommendations. Funds have been allocated to establish new activities or to purchase new instructional equipment. New courses and programs of study have been developed. New faculty and staff have been added in areas needing better support. Often the process did not discover new needs but merely documented familiar ones and placed recommendations in the appropriate administrative channels.

Without question there have also been many outcomes that have not been visible or obvious. Many changes have occurred simply because program evaluation took place. Departments have established committees to improve promotion procedures, to develop bylaws, and to review curriculum. A periodic self-evaluation requires the academic units to address and readdress questions about their role in the university community, their mission and goals, and their future needs and expectations. In sum, the evaluation process itself has often been as important to the academic unit as the final COPE report.

Administrator Evaluation System (AES). The Administrator Evaluation System is a cyclical evaluation of campus administrators, including department chairs, deans, vice-chancellors, and the chancellor. The purposes are to deliver a useful and trustworthy evaluation to the administrator to whom the person being evaluated reports, to provide information to administrators with the intent of helping them better understand their competencies as leaders, and to promote a more productive working relationship between the unit faculty and staff and the administrator being evaluated.

The information collected should relate to the effectiveness of the administrator. Effectiveness can be defined as the extent to which the administrator performs assigned and expected responsibilities and tasks. For example, information should be collected about how well the department chair or unit head recruits new faculty, handles the promotion process, and communicates faculty needs to the dean. The information should include opinions of the faculty and demographic data, such as unit success in receiving grants, student enrollment patterns, and ability to recruit new faculty. Effectiveness can also be measured by rating the administrator's style—namely, how does an administrator behave in carrying out his or her responsibilities? The *AES Catalogue of Items* includes items that cover both definitions of effectiveness.

Process. An evaluation committee is appointed by the supervisor of the administrator being evaluated. Responsibilities of the committee include meeting with the administrator being evaluated, developing an evaluation plan, designing instruments for data collection, collecting and interpreting data, and preparing a written evaluation report. The evaluation committee also meets with the supervisor to discuss contents of the evaluation report and to develop a plan to communicate to the unit faculty the procedures used in the evaluation and, at its completion, a summary of the findings.

Impact and Use. There have been many instances of department chairs and unit heads using the AES information to make improvements in their administrative performance. However, the overall net effect of administrator evaluations, more than likely, has been an increase in administrator turnover. Over the years, an increasing number of administrators have either resigned before or during the year in which they were to be evaluated. There is sufficient anecdotal information to suggest that many of these resigning administrators did not want to go through an evaluation that could be negative. In this way, the Administrator Evaluation System has provided a timely and efficient mechanism for changes in leadership.

Instructor and Course Evaluation System (ICES). ICES is a computer-based system for obtaining student ratings of instructors and courses. ICES serves two major purposes: (1) to provide information to instructors who desire to monitor and improve their instruction and (2) to provide information that others might use in promotion or similar decisions.

Faculty can select up to twenty-three items on their ICES questionnaires from a catalogue of over 600 items classified by content (course management, student outcomes, instructor characteristics and style, instructional environment, student preferences, and settings) and by specificity (global, general concepts, and specific focus). Two global items and five open-ended questions are printed on each form. The two global items are "Rate the instructor's overall teaching effectiveness" and "Rate the overall quality of the course." Also included on each form are several demographic questions (such as expected grade, elective or required course status). Departments have the option of including a set of items (the departmental core) on the forms of all faculty in the department. Faculty can also elect to include a set of six items (the student core) for which students' responses are printed in a student publication.

Process. Instructors select the questions they want to ask, and the computer prints these questions on an ICES questionnaire. Faculty administer the questionnaires during the last two weeks of classes. Results are presented in a computer-generated ICES instructor report. Presented in the report are descriptive statistics of student responses to each of the global and the twenty-three instructor-selected items. A comparison of the instructor's global item ratings with the normative ratings of the instructor's department and of the university are also provided. Faculty can elect to have the responses to the two global items sent directly to their department head or chair for administrative purposes.

Impact and Use. Faculty use of ICES questionnaires at UIUC has increased approximately 50 percent in the last ten years, from 135,557 rating forms administered in 6,103 course sections to 201,872 forms administered in 9,221 sections. There are several reasons for the increase in usage. First, there has been a steady increase over time in the number of departments that have developed departmental cores and/or required their faculty to administer ICES questionnaires.

Second, in 1987 the vice-chancellor required all assistant professors to include ICES results in promotion and tenure documentation. He based his decision on a need for more standardized or uniform information. As he wrote to faculty who wished to postpone the implementation of the requirement, "I reviewed the file of a nontenured faculty member from a unit that does not use ICES; it was impossible for me, or anyone on my staff, to be able to interpret the meaning of the scores offered from the student evaluations [submitted]."

Finally, faculty receiving exceptionally high ICES ratings are included on a list of "Excellent Teachers" that is printed in the student newspaper. The list has become a campus indication of and reward for teaching excellence, thus causing more than one associate and full professor to continue administering ICES questionnaires.

Obviously, the development of ICES has had an impact on the way faculty evaluate their teaching at UIUC. But has it had any impact on the way faculty teach? The educational specialists in our Division of Instructional Development believe that ICES has affected both faculty interest in teaching and, subsequently, the quality of teaching. The division has seen a significant increase in the number of faculty asking for help as a result of their ICES ratings. Many of these faculty work with our specialists to improve their teaching (and their ratings) and encourage others in their department to do likewise. Increased faculty interest in improving teaching has also resulted in additional requests for departmental or college workshops and seminars on teaching.

Placement and Proficiency System (P&P). UIUC administers a variety of placement tests for new freshmen in a precollege testing program. Examinations are administered on five Saturday test dates in the spring. The major purpose of the system is to help place students in the most appropriate course in each of several subject matter areas, but proficiency credit may be awarded in some areas as well.

The nationally prepared exams that are administered include the French, German, Latin, Russian, and Spanish Educational Testing Service (ETS) Achievement Tests. Students with high scores on the foreign language exams are eligible to take a departmental "validation" exam in order to qualify for proficiency credit.

The locally developed exams that are administered include mathematics (intermediate and advanced), chemistry, modern Hebrew, and a rhetoric essay exam consisting of a half-hour writing sample. Students with high scores on the rhetoric essay exam received proficiency credit (four hours) and exemption from the university rhetoric requirement.

Process. All tests in this system are available to prospective students only after they have been admitted to UIUC. Scores from the placement tests are used with admission test scores for academic advising and program planning purposes. Placement test scores do not appear on a student's official university transcript, but they are recorded and retained for college and university instructional purposes.

Impact and Use. The P&P system has been developed to assess the entering ability levels of beginning freshmen. The system helps students avoid having to review material already learned in high school or floundering in courses too difficult for their level of knowledge or preparation. As a result, students begin their college education positively by being placed into appropriate-level freshman courses, thereby enhancing their likelihood for academic success and eventual graduation.

Advanced Placement and Proficiency System (APP). The Advanced Placement Program (APP) is made available by the College Board to high school students who wish to begin college-level learning prior to entering college. Accelerated programs of study (APP courses), typically offered in the high school, prepare students to begin college course work beyond the introductory level. Students are required to complete an examination at the end of each APP course.

Currently UIUC awards proficiency credit in the following subject matter areas: art, computer science, English, French, German, Latin, Spanish, biology, chemistry, calculus, physics, music, American history, American government, and comparative government.

Process. Examinations are graded by the College Board and scores of 5 (high honors), 4 (honors), 3 (creditable), 2 (pass), or 1 (fail) are sent to the universities selected by the student. UIUC departments establish policies for awarding proficiency credit and advanced placement for each score on the five-point APP scale. UIUC recorded nationally the third highest number of examinations (4,754) submitted from May 1987 candidates.

Impact and Use. Similar to the Placement and Proficiency System, the College Board Advanced Placement Program (APP) assesses levels of student achievement in a number of content areas prior to enrollment in the university. By participating in APP, students can earn college credit for knowledge acquired in high school and/or be placed in appropriate freshman-level courses. Some beginning freshmen have earned sophomore-level status through their successful performance on APP exams.

The program is well respected and supported by the faculty. Contributing to its support on campus is the local research finding that nearly all of the students receiving APP credit at UIUC take the same number or more credit hours as do students failing to receive APP credit. The APP students fill their schedule with more elective courses, often outside of their major.

Transition Program Evaluation. Each year, UIUC admits a number of high school seniors who have academic weaknesses into the Transition Program, which provides special support through intensive academic advising and special sections of existing programs. A subgroup of these students also attend a seven-week summer program called the Summer Bridge Program. An assessment program has been developed to measure the attitudes, knowledge, and skill areas of the students in the Transition Program prior to attending the university and again at the end of each academic year.

The Educational Testing Service's Standard Test of Written English and Psychological Corporation's Stanford Diagnostic Reading Test are administered to participants, along with UIUC's rhetoric essay exam and mathematics exam.

Process. Prior to the first day of summer classes, exams are administered to students in the Bridge Program. Exam results are used to place students into appropriate sections of math and rhetoric. Group interviews are conducted with the Bridge students in the summer and again with the Transition students at the end of each academic year. The purpose of the interviews is to assess student opinion regarding academic and personal growth, attitudes toward school, and judgments of the special programs.

Impact and Use. Several campus units are responsible for parts of the Transition Program and other academic support services. Campus administration initially requested an evaluation of the program to acquire a neutral and objective assessment, primarily to make recommendations for program improvement. The eventual impact of the evaluation was the identification of several areas for program change and improvement. For example, a deficiency in the management of program information was discovered. Therefore, program strengths and weaknesses were difficult to determine since critical information, such as students' level of participation and the identification of participants and nonparticipants, was missing or impossible to find.

Also revealed were "territorial" concerns among campus units that contributed to confusion over the goals of the program and the roles it should play. An improved orientation program was also recommended to inform students of program expectations and requirements. The identification of these and other problems eventually led to several program modifications.

Campus Honors Program Evaluation. The Campus Honors Program is designed to foster close collaborative relationships between top students (104 participants in 1987) and distinguished faculty. This occurs through the small honors classes, through each student's sharing academic and research interests with his or her faculty mentor, and through the many informal contacts that grow out of the program's extracurricular offerings. An assessment component has been developed that collects information about the motivational characteristics of the honors students, their academic and nonacademic experiences, and the types of activities in which they participated while enrolled at UIUC.

The College Student Experiences Survey (CSES) is administered to learn how students spend their time—in course work, in the library, in contacts with faculty, in extracurricular activities, in various social and cultural activities, and in taking advantage of other facilities and opportunities that exist in the college setting. SPECTRUM is used to measure the motivational characteristics of the honors students. This instrument measures four basic motivational factors: accomplishment, recognition, power, and affiliation. Also administered are group interviews and an opinion survey, both designed to assess student opinions regarding academic and personal development, attitudes toward school, and judgments of the honors program.

Process. The CSES and opinion survey are administered at the end of each academic year. Group interviews are also conducted during the last two to three weeks of a semester within honors classes and in specially arranged small groups, such as an Honors Program pizza party. Evaluation results are given to the program administrator to indicate program strengths and weaknesses and to suggest areas for improvement.

Impact and Use. Of all the assessment programs discussed, the evaluation of the Campus Honors Program has had the least impact. There is a good explanation for this: The program has required only minor modification. Students and faculty alike spoke highly of the program. The few recommendations passed on to the program dealt with making a good program even better. The strongest recommendation (adopted by program administrators) was to refrain from housing honors students together in the same residence hall. Nearly all of the honors students expressed concern over being set apart from the other students. In the words of one student, "You want us to buy T-shirts that say 'HONORS STUDENT,' too." While the evaluation had little to improve on, the overall positive evaluation of the program is continually considered by administrators when they speak proudly of the "well-received" Campus Honors Program.

International Teaching Assistant (ITA) Assessment and Training Program. In 1987 the state legislature passed state of Illinois law 1516, which requires all state universities to "establish programs which will ensure that all their classroom instructors will possess oral proficiency in the English language." To respond to the law, we have initiated an assessment program for international students in which all graduate students who are not native English speakers and who are planning to teach at UIUC are required to pass a test of spoken English and attend a teaching skills orientation program before they begin providing instruction.

For this assessment program, the Test of Spoken English (TSE), developed by ETS, or its institutional version, SPEAK, is administered. Student feedback surveys and classroom observations are also conducted.

Process. All non-native-English-speaking graduate students who wish to be employed as teaching assistants (TAs) at UIUC must pass either the Test of Spoken English or SPEAK with a score of 230 or higher. An appeals process is provided. Individuals who fail to demonstrate oral proficiency are required to participate in at least one semester of ongoing campus improvement activities before they can retake SPEAK.

Individuals who demonstrate oral proficiency must attend a weeklong campuswide teaching skills orientation before they begin providing instruction. Once in a teaching assignment, the international TA must be monitored by the academic unit in which he or she is hired. International TAs are also required to distribute and collect student feedback surveys at the end of the first three weeks of the first semester in which they provide instruction.

Impact and Use. In 1988 there were 2,147 graduate student teaching assistants at UIUC of which 563 were not U.S. citizens. Excluding the seventy-three international teaching assistants (TAs) teaching foreign languages (and not required to take the SPEAK assessment), 97 percent of the 563 ITAs were administered SPEAK or the TSE assessment. As a result of the testing, forty-seven ITAs participated in the 1988 fall orientation.

Since the fall assessment and orientation program, there has been a marked decrease in the number of complaints and the types of complaints by 1988 undergraduate students regarding their ITA's ability to speak English. In the College of Commerce, for instance, there were only three such complaints by undergraduates this fall compared to more than a dozen each semester in previous years. Two of the complaints were not concerning the TA's inability to "speak" English but rather his or her inability to "converse" in English. In the case of the third complaint, the complaining student finally admitted that he just did not want an ITA.

Every academic unit with whom our office has communicated regarding explanations of the law and UIUC policy has expressed gratitude for the assessment program. Before the policy was enacted, many units reported feeling a responsibility to give appointments to everyone. They now report having this pressure almost entirely removed because of the assessment program. A further impact is apparent as academic units are changing the focus of their concerns about those ITAs who are eligible to teach. With the added confidence that oral English is not an issue, some unit heads and department chairs are adding measures that address the benefits of their ITA to the international components of an undergraduate education. The head of business administration, for example, on the first day of classes will introduce, in person, each ITA in his department. Each introduction will include the advantages of an ITA, the qualifications of each ITA, and the problems that the undergraduates admittedly might experience.

Most of the academic units have responded to the ITA policy by rescinding the teaching appointments for those ITAs who do not pass SPEAK. In all cases the units have found other monies to support these ITAs for the length of the teaching appointment. While it was somewhat difficult for the units to find suitable replacements for these ITAs the week before classes began, they reported that this was a marked improvement over having to respond to students' complaints after classes had begun. Units that had to do this are presently being more emphatic to prospective ITAs about the oral English proficiency requirement. They are able to insist on the SPEAK assessment before they offer teaching appointments.

Enrollment in the English as a Second Language (ESL 406) course has doubled over the past year (from twenty students to fifty-eight students) and from one course a semester to two courses plus one course in the summer session. Additionally, there have been one to two fully enrolled IMS/Department of English as an International Language (DEIL) workshop series each semester since the enactment of the policy. Before that time, there was only one, and it had an enrollment of four ITAs.

In summary, the impact of the policy and law is felt in the increased participation in the orientations, in the number of SPEAK assessments, in the increased enrollment in the ESL courses and semester workshops, in the academic units' statements of satisfaction regarding the law and policy and their ability to handle a problem before classes begin, and in the new focus of the support of academic units for the ITAs who are eligible to teach. UIUC can feel confident that its policy is responding effectively to the law and that it has taken a major step in assuring undergraduates that their ITAs are orally proficient in English.

Math Statewide Testing Program. The Illinois Universities Test of College Preparatory Mathematics is a diagnostic test of college preparatory mathematics designed for college-intending high school juniors.

The testing program is a cooperative project of the mathematics departments of all of the state universities in Illinois and is available to all Illinois high schools. It is designed to help students assess their progress in preparing themselves for college-level mathematics and to encourage them to take any additional mathematics courses that they need during their senior year in high school.

The Illinois Universities Test of College Preparatory Mathematics was developed by a committee of math faculty from several of the state universities in Illinois. The test package consists of three sets of multiple-choice items. Parts one and two cover beginning algebra, geometry, and the first semester of advanced algebra. Part three covers trigonometry and exponentials and the second semester of advanced algebra.

Process. In 1988, approximately 450 (50 percent) Illinois high schools and 45,000 students voluntarily participated in the program. Participating high schools administer parts one and two of the test, which cover math usually completed by college-bound students by the middle of the junior year, to juniors sometime in January or early February. Cumulative school reports and individual student reports are returned to a test coordinator at each school by late February. Included in the individual reports are recommendations (based on test results) for further study of mathematics during the senior year. The cumulative school reports can be used by high schools to assess the overall performance of their students. No comparisons between high schools are compiled or reported.

Impact and Use. The testing program is in its fourth year of statewide operation. It appears to be having several effects in the participating schools. Approximately 34 percent of the participating high schools report that more seniors are taking a math course during their final year in high school. In addition, 28 percent of the participating schools are offering new courses that are specifically designed to help students whose algebra and geometry skills are not adequate for introductory college-level math.

At UIUC there has been a significant drop in the number of entering freshmen who are required to take a remedial math course. In the fall of 1986, 525 students were placed in remedial math courses as a result of low math placement test scores, as compared to the previous year's 850 students. This trend has continued over the past three years. In addition, the number of freshmen entering UIUC with Advanced Placement Program credit in calculus has increased from 700 to approximately 1,000 per year. This latter result is partially due to a number of high schools adding APP calculus to the curriculum in order to accommodate student requests for an additional math course in the senior year.

Meeting the Need for Information to Improve Campus Policy Making

As identified in Figure 1, there are at least five major campus needs addressed by and eight major uses made of one or more of the nine programs discussed. Of foremost concern is a need for information about quality. There are campus needs to collect information about the quality of campus units and academic departments. For example, information collected during a COPE procedure about departmental quality is often used to make improvements in the curriculum, course offerings, and teaching assignments. COPE information is also used by central administration to make budgetary and staffing decisions.

Departmental administrators need information about the effectiveness of their faculty (ICES results) in order to make decisions regarding rank, salary, and teaching assignments. The administrator evaluations provide information regarding the effectiveness of department and unit heads and chairs and are used by central administration to make retention or dismissal decisions. UIUC student recruiters use information about the success or failure of special academic programs such as the Honors and Transition Programs in their recruitment of special populations. The central administration also uses the same program information to make program support decisions. Finally, students rely heavily on placement testing information (P&P and Mathematics Statewide Testing) in their selection of courses and sometimes major fields of study.

Assessment of General Education or Learning Outcomes

Before concluding this chapter on evaluation and assessment activities at UIUC, I would like to comment on an area that obviously has not been directly addressed—the assessment of general education or learning outcomes of undergraduates. To date there are no formal programs designed to assess the achievement or learning outcomes of our students. Once students begin course work at UIUC, the only tests they take are classroom examinations. UIUC, like many other large research universities (Ory and Parker, 1988), does not conduct value-added analyses of student outcomes or conduct junior-year general education testing such as junior rising exams, ACT's COMP, or ETS's Academic Profile.

The evaluation programs described in this chapter reflect a "project-based" approach to assessment similar to the strategy followed at Harvard University. Conducting "do-able" assessments related to clearly definable projects or programs for the purpose of improvement or policy decisions is the approach, rather than large-scale measurement of amorphous objects such as general education. However, in reading a draft of this chapter, one of our associate vice-chancellors was distressed to read that UIUC was not assessing general education outcomes. "What do you mean we are not assessing these outcomes? Of course we are!" was the exact response.

The associate vice-chancellor went on to describe several activities that involve the assessment of general education outcomes. Beginning this fall, students are asked to respond to several items concerning general education as part of the COPE process. The regular alumni survey also contains questions bearing on general education, including questions about satisfaction with and quality of the students' UIUC program of study. Alumni placement rates, both in jobs and in graduate and professional programs, are another form of regularly collected assessment information. Also cited were several campus committees studying and assessing the need for much expanded campuswide general education requirements and the evaluation of teaching at UIUC. All of these examples do indeed indicate UIUC interest in assessing the growth and development of students, but they also reveal a reluctance to define assessment of general education outcomes as the administration of tests other than those administered by professors in their courses.

Conclusion

For our particular higher education setting, different audiences have unique needs for and make different use of assessment information collected from multiple sources through a variety of methods. Through time, our campus audiences have become dependent on the information collected in the nine evaluation programs for making campus decisions, whether they are students selecting courses or administrators awarding promotions. Thus, our office has seen how assessment information collected in a systematic, fair, and credible manner can be useful for campus decision making. I believe that our evaluation programs have addressed Harvard President Derek Bok's concern that a primary goal of assessment research is "to persuade a skeptical academic audience that research can make a real contribution to concrete policy choices" (communication to Professor Richard Light, February 18, 1988).

References

Brandenburg, D. C., Braskamp, L. A., and Ory, J. C. "Considerations for an Evaluation Program of Instructional Quality." *Center on Evaluation and Development and Research Quarterly*, 1979, *12*, 8-12.

Braskamp, L. A., Brandenburg, D. C., and Ory, J. C. *Evaluating Teaching Effectiveness: A Guidebook*. Newbury Park, Calif.: Sage, 1984.

Ory, J. C., and Parker, S. A. "Survey of Assessment Activities at Large Research Universities." Paper presented at the annual meeting of the American Evaluation Association, New Orleans, October 1988.

Popham, W. J. "Toward Orthodoxy: Ten Commandments for Educational Evaluators." Paper presented at the annual meeting of the American Educational Research Association, Washington, D.C., March 1975.

John C. Ory is acting director of the Office of Instructional and Management Services and associate professor of educational psychology at the University of Illinois, Urbana-Champaign.

In order to be responsive to the great variety of issues currently facing higher education, assessment must have a correspondingly broad definition.

Improving Higher Education: The Need for a Broad View of Assessment

Peter J. Gray, Robert M. Diamond

The current assessment movement has as its primary goal the improvement of higher education. Of course, improvement does not happen by chance. Rather, it requires an institutional commitment to change, the availability of quality information to inform decisions, and the willingness to commit the resources needed to collect this information and to make the identified changes. The key element is quality information. Information quality is often judged by its utility—that is, the extent to which it addresses the specific needs of users. A logical and sequential process will enhance the potential of collecting quality information and of utilizing it appropriately.

Such a process, whether appearing under the name of assessment, evaluation, program review, strategic planning, or policy analysis, contains the same essential elements (see Figure 1). This process begins with the clarification of the reasons for conducting a study and ends with the utilization of information as the basis for establishing and implementing plans for change. The use of a comprehensive process like that shown in Figure 1 can lead to the proper balanced focus of the whys, whats, and hows of assessment noted by Ewell (1987).

P. J. Gray (ed.). *Achieving Assessment Goals Using Evaluation Techniques.*
New Directions for Higher Education, no. 67. San Francisco: Jossey-Bass, Fall 1989.

Figure 1. Systematic Data Collection: The Essential Elements

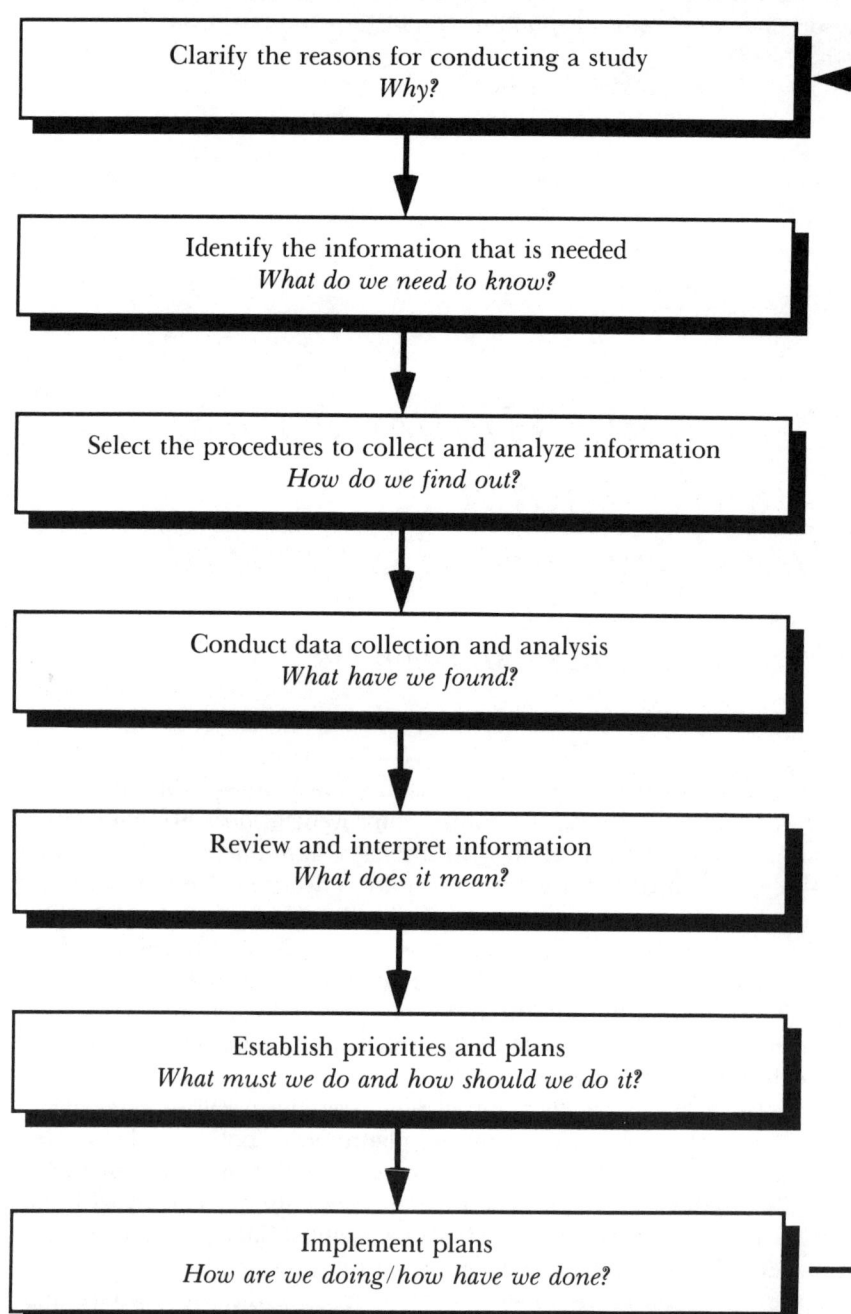

An important but often overlooked facet of the process shown in Figure 1 is that clients are involved to the extent that they desire in each of its elements, thus enhancing their feeling of ownership. Client involvement in the design and implementation of a study, in the interpretation of the results, in the establishment of priorities and plans, and in subsequent implementation of those plans also addresses many of the concerns raised by other authors in this sourcebook. These include: the organizational realities that temper assessment practice that are noted by Sell; the "So, what's the use?" issues raised by Braskamp; the considerations described by Ory; as well as Dennison and Bunda's premises of practice.

In recognition of the need for systematically collected information relative to many different concerns, colleges and universities have established agencies charged with providing support to meet this need. The authors in this sourcebook are connected with such offices. They have conducted studies that range from ongoing course evaluations to studies of program effectiveness to measuring institutionwide minority student retention.

A case in point is the evaluation and research unit of the Syracuse University Center for Instructional Development. As a support unit to the university, the center designs and conducts studies at the request of many different academic units and administrative offices. Using the process shown in Figure 1, the center provides information relative to courses, curricula, academic and nonacademic programs, academic and nonacademic administrative concerns, and institutional issues (Figure 2). Depending on the reason for conducting a study and the type of information needed, the center employs various data collection techniques, such as testing, surveying, reviewing existing records, meta-analysis, interviewing, observation, and content analysis. Information is collected from students, faculty, staff, administrators, parents, alumni, and employers, as appropriate.

A centralized office that conducts studies relative to all areas can be extremely valuable in helping to avoid duplication of effort by coordinating study implementation and fostering the integration of study findings. Having a centralized office is also cost-effective since it permits specialized talents to be used campuswide, thus reducing the need to add evaluation and research specialists to many different campus units. A significant aspect of the Syracuse University center is that it also contains an instructional development unit. The combination of an evaluation/research unit and an instructional development unit facilitates the use of information in the resolution of problems that have been identified. (For a description of the integration of both areas within a single center, see Diamond, 1989.)

The examples included in the following discussion describe the role of the evaluation and research unit, its interaction with the development unit of the center, and the interrelationships that exist among the areas in Figure 2.

Courses, Curricula, and Programs

"Assessment per se guarantees nothing by way of improvement. . . . Only when used in *combination* with good instruction . . . , in a *program* of improvement, can the device strengthen education" (Marchese, 1987, p. 8).

Without a wide variety of data, those involved directly in courses, curricula, and programs can find themselves basing decisions on incomplete and, therefore, potentially misleading information. As a result, their efforts may end up wasting resources and having far less impact than if a wide range of quality information is available.

In our definition, courses can include, among others: traditional credit-bearing, discipline-based offerings such as introductory psychology and economics; extracurricular courses such as career exploration; and focused skill-building courses such as resource utilization and problem solving. Courses may be organized as lectures, laboratories, workshops, independent study, programmed instruction, seminars, internships, and so on. Curricula are sets of courses related to a single discipline, such as a biology undergraduate curriculum, or to a group of disciplines, such as a master's in business administration (MBA) curriculum. Programs are combinations of elements that may or may not include courses. Examples are: an honors program consisting of special sections of courses; a campuswide teaching assistant orientation program including lectures, work-

Figure 2. Study Focus Areas

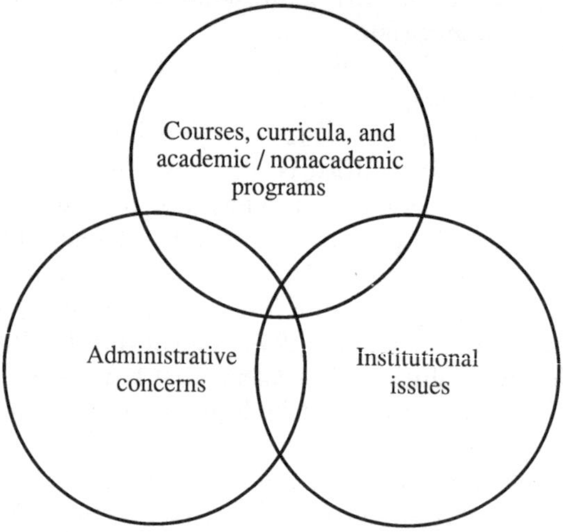

shops, field trips, information sessions, and social events; a program to support minority students in the sciences and professional areas featuring study groups, tutoring, career exploration opportunities, off-campus retreats, and mentoring by faculty and staff; and a student development program in the residence halls involving informal and formal activities for individuals, small groups, and large groups.

At Syracuse University, studies related to the development of new or to the improvement of existing courses, curricula, and programs are guided by the summary model shown in Figure 3; the full model is in Diamond (1989). Each development step has a related data collection component. In the first step, project selection, data are collected from faculty, students, and others to determine the nature of the problem and the attention it warrants. From an administrative perspective, this step aids in the establishment of priorities relative to the selection of projects for action. Most important problems are often identified by more than one source of data. Without this wide range of supportive data, priorities could not be established and major problems would continue to exist without being addressed.

Step two of the model, the collection of basic input data, provides the information needed by a development team to create the ideal design of the course, curriculum, or program. The center's development staff facilitates the creation of the ideal design. In addition to a more detailed analysis of the information collected as part of step one, basic input data may

Figure 3. Course, Curriculum, and Program Development Data

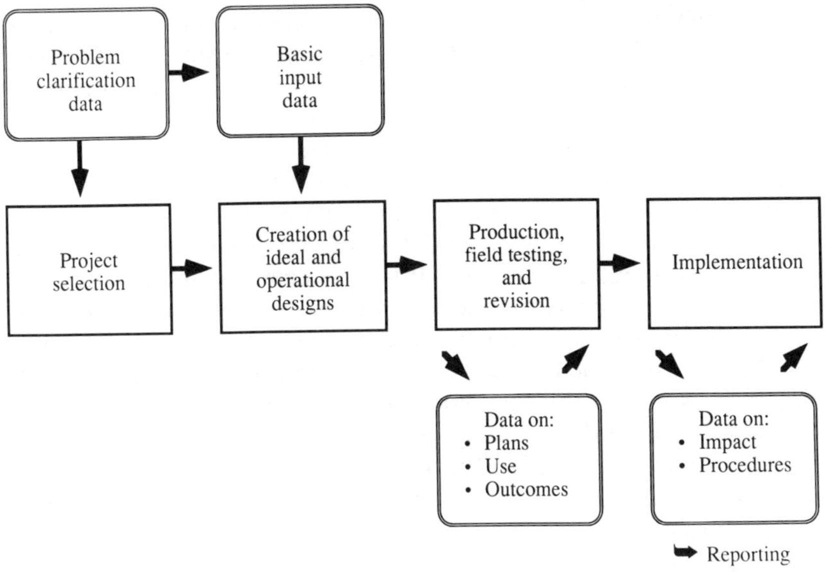

be gathered in relation to the relevant content area; the participant's prior knowledge, skills, and attitudes; faculty assumptions; student priorities; societal needs; relevant research in the field of study and in instructional development; and institutional priorities. This information is used to design the sequence that would ideally solve the problems stimulating the development effort. Experience has shown that thinking in the ideal forces those responsible for courses, curricula, or programs to test assumptions, explore options, and address key issues that would otherwise be ignored.

To create the operational version of the design, the staff uses additional information on available resources (human, time, material, facilities, financial), actual number of people likely to participate, and institutional constraints such as grading policies and scheduling limitations. In effect, an understanding of the real-world context guides the evolution of the design from the ideal course, curriculum, or program, which was initially conceptualized, into one that can be realized within this context. In some cases the context will necessitate a modification of the ideal. In other cases, the real world can be modified so that the ideal can be more fully realized.

The production, field testing, and revision step requires the collection of information about the development of materials and procedures, the use of materials and implementation of procedures, and the resulting outcomes. Content analysis techniques are used to verify the consistency of materials and procedures with each other and with the goals and objectives of the designs. Documenting the use of materials and procedures provides the basis for determining the causes of outcomes. Using item analysis techniques to monitor the results of quizzes and exams can provide data on the accomplishment of specific outcomes by particular groups. Collecting these data during the field test step is particularly important so that sound information is available to guide the revision of the activities and materials before full implementation.

Data collected during the implementation step focuses on the short-term and long-term achievement associated with participation in the course, curriculum, or program. In addition, procedural aspects are monitored to ensure that they do not stray too far from the original plan without well-thought-out reasons. It is these data that are used for external reporting and to identify the areas where continued work is required.

The following are examples of how these steps are implemented. The first concerns the redesign of a micro- and macroeconomics course sequence, and the other concerns the development of a campuswide teaching-assistant orientation program.

Micro- and Macroeconomics. The redesign of a micro- and macroeconomics course sequence began with the identification of this course as "having problems" over a period of time. Students and parents continuously reported concerns about the high failure rate in the course, faculty turnover was constant, and the course was rarely the same from one year to the next. However, some very important changes had recently occurred that brought the problems into sharp focus and that suggested that major improvements would be supported.

The problems were pinpointed through focused discussions with relevant faculty and a survey of current students. Together they identified problems in each of the following areas: text and readings; the exams, tests, and quizzes; the homework assignments; and the organization of the large-group presentations. Also indicated were a willingness by the department to hire a new faculty member to take responsibility for the course redesign effort and a willingness by the university to expend the other resources needed to make changes.

A key factor in deciding to pursue this project was the departmental commitment to assign a faculty member to the course for a number of years. As a result, the problems seemed fixable and the potential for success seemed to exist. Therefore, the project was selected for action as a joint effort between the department and the Center for Instructional Development. The center's role was to provide instructional development, evaluation, and production staff. A department faculty member provided context expertise.

In addition to the information gathered as part of the problem clarification step, four sets of basic input data were collected: (1) the reasons that students were taking the course; (2) where they were from (that is, their department or program); (3) their ability in the mathematics, algebra, and geometry skills that were needed for success in these courses; and (4) the assumptions that faculty had regarding these prerequisite skills. Through the student survey, it was learned that a sizable number of students were taking the course because there was no other basic economics course available to meet the requirement of their major, which was outside of economics. Review of a special test administered at the beginning of one semester revealed that a large number of the students did not have the algebra or geometry skills that were needed for success, which had been assumed by the faculty. Together with the information about the problem, these basic input data led to the design of an ideal program that was refined into an operational sequence. As Diamond (1989) states: "At some point in the development process, the preliminary or 'ideal' instructional design phase is completed, and modifications begin to meet the practical limitations of the real world. This transformation from the 'ideal' to the 'real' is gradual and, in reality, it is impossible to identify the point at which one stage ends and another begins" (p. 102).

The final design guided the development of a course manual; a diagnostic test and remedial instruction in relevant mathematics, algebra, and geometry topics; and a separate introductory economics course for nonmajors. These newly developed components were field-tested over a two-year period. Feedback from exams and quizzes, midsemester and end-of-semester student surveys, and reviews by the instructor and teaching assistants helped refine them so that, to the extent possible, reality approximated the ideal. It is interesting to note that the new economics course for nonmajors has continued to expand in enrollment.

Subsequent implementation has continued to be monitored. The course components have been fine-tuned, and new problem areas (such as the selection of teaching assistants) have been identified and dealt with as appropriate.

Teaching Assistant Orientation Program. A second example concerns the development of a new teaching assistant orientation program at Syracuse University. This program supports the academic mission of the institution by helping to prepare new teaching assistants for their various responsibilities.

A national study of teaching assistants was conducted in the spring of 1986 (Diamond and Gray, 1987). At Syracuse and other institutions issues were identified relative to teaching responsibilities, the supervision of teaching assistants, and special international teaching assistant concerns. Data from many different sources helped to clarify the issues and confirmed that this was a project worth pursuing. These sources included the national study, earlier research at Syracuse University, a report by the Syracuse University graduate board, a set of priorities established by the academic deans, and information from teaching assistants, concerned faculty, and administrators. Key to the decision to proceed and to the ultimate success of the program was a commitment of support received from Syracuse University's vice-president for undergraduate studies and the vice-president for graduate studies and research.

The design process included the collection of information by development staff from each school and college at the university. Meetings were held with people who had been responsible for previous local orientations. An evaluation task force was formed to develop and implement a comprehensive evaluation study that had as its goals: (1) to provide feedback to those conducting the orientation for purposes of improvement; (2) to determine the immediate and long-term impact of the orientation on teaching assistants; and (3) to collect information useful in describing the orientation to external audiences. In order to reach these goals, ten different data collection methods were used. Some occurred concurrent with the orientation (teaching assistant interviews), some occurred both before and after the orientation (annual teaching assistant survey), and some occurred only after the orientation (administer and faculty follow-up interviews).

Information collected relative to the first offering of the orientation in August 1988, which may be viewed as the field-test step, suggested changes to be made in preparation for the August 1989 offering, the full implementation. The evaluation continues in a modified form in order to provide information on the impact of the orientation and to provide feedback on its implementation (Rogler and Gray, 1989).

The provision of quality information was an important ingredient in the success of these and other course, curriculum, and program development projects.

Administrative Concerns

"Even if assessment were to identify previously unrecognized deficiencies, correction would require more than pedagogical or curricular tinkering" (Molotsky, 1988, p. 4).

Collecting data relative to various courses, curricula, and programs is a major responsibility of the center's evaluation and research unit. However, administrative concerns and institutional issues also demand considerable attention.

To the extent that administrators are responsible for the creation of new or the improvement of existing courses, curricula, or programs, such development may be described as an administrative concern. This overlap is shown in Figure 1. However, as Figure 1 also suggests, administrative concerns cover much more than this. An academic department chair, for example, is not only concerned with the development of the academic content and instructional procedures of the department but he or she must also identify and resolve problems related to physical facilities, the provision of services, and staffing, which may or may not be directly related to instruction. Similarly, nonacademic department heads are concerned both with the programmatic elements of their department and with facilities, services, and staffing. The Center for Instructional Development's evaluation and research unit has conducted studies that provide information to help identify and resolve both academic and nonacademic administrative concerns.

Physical Facilities. Physical facilities include classrooms, office space, laboratories, residence and dining halls, recreational areas, health centers, bookstores, and student centers. Administrative concerns in this regard focus on the availability of certain types of space, the condition of facilities, the actual and potential use of existing facilities, and the need for remodeling or adding to those facilities. The following are examples of the types of studies conducted by the center for numerous administrative offices relative to physical facilities.

Student Center. In recent years a variety of studies have focused on the new Syracuse University student center and its related physical facilities (lounges, dining hall, bookstore, game room, nightclub). One study, involving a set of on-site surveys of those who use the center, has been conducted twice yearly since the center opened in 1985. These surveys have both a common core of items that provide consistent data across spaces and specific items related to concerns of those responsible for individual spaces. These repeated surveys allow important changes in student perceptions to be identified, appropriate changes to be made, and the impact of changes to be documented. (A similar on-site survey process is under way regarding the university health center.)

One area of the student center where this information has had an especially noticeable impact is the student nightclub. From the time the student center first opened, the results of the on-site survey had indicated dissatisfaction with this space. To understand better the causes of dissatisfaction, the research team held a series of student group discussions to gather suggestions for changes. Most of the recommended changes involved the physical structure and appearance of the nightclub. As a result of this input, the entire ground floor of the student center was redesigned and remodeled, including the nightclub, game room, and lounge area. Subsequent surveys have shown a marked increase in satisfaction with the entire area.

Campus Recreation Facilities. In collecting data to inform decisions about the need for expanded recreational facilities at Syracuse University, recreation staff counted how many people were able to use the facilities and how many people were waiting to use them on different days and at different times.

A survey based on a stratified random sample of all full-time students was also conducted by the evaluation and research unit to determine what off-campus alternatives people had found due to the lack of on-campus facilities. This survey provided information about potential use that was not directly observable through the counting procedures. Together the observations and the survey data were used to make the case to the university administration that new recreation facilities were needed. These facilities are currently under construction.

Academic Space. A survey of all academic spaces (classrooms, meeting rooms, laboratories, offices) was conducted at the request of the central administration to provide an inventory of various spaces and their current condition. Literally every instructional space on campus was examined by people who checked the seating, lighting, audiovisual capabilities, electrical outlets, and so on, and reported their condition. Faculty and staff also reported their perceptions of office and other relevant spaces. This information was used to set priorities for adding and refurbishing spaces. For example, projection television units and upgraded sound systems were added to a number of large instructional spaces. The findings of this study are also being used to justify additional office and other space and to provide guidelines for all new classroom designs.

Off-Campus Housing. At the request of a university senate committee, a survey was conducted of all students living in off-campus housing (primarily apartments within a mile of the university). Students were asked to rate the quality of their housing, the responsiveness of landlords, and the problems they had encountered. Results were summarized by the landlord and reported back to the student-run agency that helps students find off-campus housing and deal with problems. To meet the needs identified in this study, the student-run agency has created a number of publications for students who are looking for off-campus housing.

Services. In addition to facilities concerns, administrators also worry about services in regard to the way students and other clients are treated (in other words, the quality of services) and the range of services provided. Academic services include, among others, academic advising, course registration, and academic computing. Nonacademic services include, for example, housing services, health services, dining services, and financial aid. The following examples illustrate the diversity of studies conducted at Syracuse University to address administrative concerns regarding services.

Student Nightclub. Along with the need for changes in the physical aspects of the nightclub, there was a perceived need to increase the diversity of student programs. The management staff worked hard to accomplish this, and, as a result, this space has become very popular with a wide variety of students. In fact, some management concerns have arisen due to this popularity. Therefore, recently a second set of focused interviews was held to gather information on service concerns, such as scheduling of events, provision of security, and admission policies. This information will help to refine the management of nightclub events in the future.

Office Atmosphere. At the request of a university senate committee and with the cooperation of the university's Human Resources Division, a study is currently being designed to assess the quality of interactions that students experience in various academic and administrative offices. A stratified random sample of students is being selected to provide input on their school or college dean's office and their departmental office. In addition, they will be asked to comment on other offices that they regularly interact with (such as financial aid, registrar, placement, residence services). The results of the study will be reported back to the senate committee and the Human Resources Division so that they can recognize offices that are doing a good job and identify those where improvements are needed.

Staffing. One of the most important administrative concerns is staffing. More specifically this concern includes: (1) the enhancement of performance (developmental or formative concerns); (2) hiring, retention, annual review, promotion, merit pay, and tenure (comparative or summative concerns); and (3) how staff may best be deployed (utilization concerns). Quality data about staff capabilities can yield important information to both the individual staff member and the administrator by supplying data about the individual's strengths and weaknesses. When gathered early enough, this information furnishes the basis for improvement—that is, it can be used in a formative sense. When gathered over time, in a consistent manner, it can provide a range of supportive material for summative decisions and for staff utilization decisions.

A review of the literature suggests seven characteristics that contribute to effective instruction (Centra, Froh, Gray, and Lambert, 1987). A generic form of this list can be used with both instructional and noninstructional staff (Figure 4). Using these characteristics, systems have been designed to provide information for developmental, comparative, and utilization purposes. The publication by Centra, Froh, Gray, and Lambert has been made available through the center to academic offices throughout the university and is given to each new faculty member as part of an orientation program.

If the purpose of the assessment is primarily developmental, then the individual should have the major say in determining the characteristics considered, the questions asked, and how data are collected, analyzed, and reported. In fact, at the Center for Instructional Development, data collected for developmental purposes are shared only with the individual involved, who then decides if he or she wishes to share it with others.

Staff often want to collect information relative to specific topics, such as those identified as weaknesses through standardized evaluation instruments. They also want feedback on specific materials that they have developed or methods they have used. Such information can be obtained in a variety of ways. Specially designed surveys or focused dialogues with students or other clients are used to elicit comments and suggestions about materials and methods. Structured reviews by colleagues identify the strengths and weaknesses of the materials or methods. The careful review of outcomes on tests and other instruments indicates the impact of the materials and methods. Lists of various data collection techniques and those who can provide information are also included in Figure 4.

If information is to be used to make comparative decisions, then a framework needs to be established to ensure that all cases have the same type of information. In this regard, the characteristics shown in Figure 4 can be used to designate categories of information to be collected relative to all those being compared. For example, a common evaluation form could be developed for use within a department. Such a form would have items under each of the characteristics. The form would be administered on a regular basis. The results, which indicate in a general way areas of strength and weakness, could become part of a staff member's portfolio of information relative to his or her effectiveness. It is very important that individuals feel that the common data collected are relevant to them and that they have an opportunity to influence the data's interpretation.

Figure 4. Characteristics That Contribute to Course, Curriculum, or Program Effectiveness

What

- Good organization of content, materials, and methods
- Effective communication
- Sufficient knowledge of and enthusiasm for subject
- Positive attitudes toward clients, for example, students
- Appropriateness of anticipated outcomes
- Fairness in the implementation of procedures including the assessment of outcomes
- Flexibility in approaches

Who

- Self
- Colleagues
- Current clients/students and alumni
- Administrators

How

- Log, journal
- Guided observation
- Structured interview
- Survey/questionnaire
- Test or appraisal
- Content analysis

Source: Centra, Froh, Gray, and Lambert, 1987.

The unique information gathered for developmental purposes might be summarized and included in a performance portfolio along with commonly collected material. The unique information elaborates on that provided by a common means and sets a context within which the commonly collected information can be interpreted. For example, in the case of weaknesses identified through a common measure, it can illustrate attempts to remedy them. The common information, in turn, provides an external reference point for judging the unique information and for making comparisons.

The information gained in formative and summative evaluations provides the basis for making decision about the utilization of staff for various assignments. For example, a faculty member may have indicated a desire to work on a certain course sequence, and over time she or he may have developed some very successful materials. This information should be brought to bear on staffing decisions. In nonacademic situations, a staff member may have demonstrated leadership capabilities that recommend her or him to fill a staff vacancy.

The following examples illustrate the use of systematically collected data to address staffing concerns.

Teaching Assistant Supervision. Several Syracuse University courses, including the economics courses already mentioned, use a variety of assessment methods to monitor teaching assistant performance. One is a consistent midterm and end-of-term student course evaluation survey. The information from the survey is reported for each teaching assistant. The faculty members responsible for the courses and the lead teaching assistants also observe each of the teaching assistants several times during the semester. In addition, section-by-section results on the major exams and quizzes are compared to determine if there are differences in student learning relative to various sections. During the year this information is used for developmental purposes to help teaching assistants improve their teaching. At the end of the year it is used to help decide which teaching assistants should be hired for the following year and what their assignments should be.

Reverse Review. Each year, two student services administrators use a common form to collect data from those whom they supervise regarding the administrators' performance. The anonymity of respondents is facilitated by having Center for Instructional Development evaluation and research staff compile and report the results. This review has led to the improvement of relationships between these administrators and their supervisees.

While many studies involving facilities, services, and staff are conducted to address the concerns of individual offices, others have institutional implications.

Institutional Issues

"The level of institutional quality depends not only on an institution's educational processes and resources but also on the institution's successful use of those processes and resources to achieve established goals" (Southern Association of Colleges and Schools, 1988, p. 13).

Institutional issues are those concerns that have institutionwide implications, even though they may be related to courses, curricula, and programs or to academic and nonacademic facilities, services, and staff. For example, if there are concerns that a particular academic course, academic support program, or nonacademic facility is related to student attrition, then this concern raises institutional issues. Studies at this level may be designed to address issues of institutional problem clarification, planning, or impact using the essential elements in Figure 1.

The undergraduate student retention and attrition project at Syracuse University provides a multifaceted example of how institutional issues can be addressed using these elements. The components of this project, which are discussed in the following examples, fall under the jurisdiction of the members of a committee headed by the vice-president for undergraduate studies. Some components are the individual responsibility of a committee member, and others involve the committee collectively.

Problem Clarification. The stimulus for the first component of the retention and attrition project was a clear concern with the retention rate of students in general and of minority students in particular. Information previously gathered formally and informally from students, faculty, and staff had indicated concerns about the university's policies and practices in the area of retention. However, clarification was needed in the form of comprehensive, longitudinal, quantitative data on student persistence and graduation rates. Clarification of these institutional issues was the reason *why* information was needed (element one in Figure 1).

The specific information needed for problem clarification was described in relation to a set of questions. These questions included: What mutually exclusive categories can be developed to describe students' status at the university over time? What demographic and other student-related variables can be used in the analysis of the data relative to subpopulations? How should intrauniversity transfers be described? How can data be displayed to be most understandable?

In response to these questions, data were collected on cohorts of students beginning with the freshmen who entered the university in the fall of 1980. For each semester up to the present, the status of each cohort was determined regarding those students who were continuous registrants and who had never had a change of status, those who had returned after stopping out, those who for that semester at least had stopped out but who would later return, those who had left the university and not returned, and those students who had graduated.

These data were obtained through an analysis of information in the university's student record system data base. The results were organized into reports that showed the status of the cohorts in regard to these five categories from the time they entered the university to the present. In addition, other relevant variables were included in the study—for example, gender, ethnicity, school or college, grade point average, financial aid patterns, and intrauniversity transfer.

A detailed picture of attrition and retention at Syracuse University was created as a result of this problem clarification process. For example, high attrition rates were found to be associated with certain semesters. It was discovered that various groups had different attrition rates and patterns of attrition. Some factors were discovered to have a positive and others a negative influence on attrition.

Our understanding of retention and attrition is being refined continually. For example, the way new cohorts of students differ from older cohorts is revealed as additional time is added to their history. New variables are being defined, and their relationships to the retention and attrition data are being explored. And ways are being devised to account for students' social and academic integration as factors in retention and attrition.

Planning. A number of high-priority areas were identified based on retention and attrition patterns and the perceived influence of different factors. The priorities were related to such areas as admissions, orientation, residential life, academic life, and student support. In many cases the model shown in Figure 3 was or currently is being used to develop programs to accomplish these priorities. Within the context of this model, information gained regarding retention and attrition is used to select projects for action. Additional base data are collected to guide the development of the ideal and real program sequences. In many cases, information is collected during the field test of programs, and, as will be described in the next section, data are collected regarding their impact. The following are some examples of institutionwide planning projects in which the center is involved.

Admissions. An admissions priority was to widen the pool of potential freshmen and especially minorities. To address this issue, a program called the Syracuse Challenge was proposed as a way to encourage Syracuse City School District students to enter the university. This partnership between the university and the school district guarantees students who have met established criteria academic support in high school, admission to the university, and financial support based on need during their undergraduate career at Syracuse University.

Orientation. Another priority suggested by the retention and attrition data involved freshmen orientation. Based on the definition of orientation as the ongoing integration of students into the university community, a program is being designed to help students make the initial transition from high school to college and also to support their development throughout their college careers. In addition, the orientation program has as its theme "Community through individuality." This theme will be carried out through many activities designed to help students retain their individuality, appreciate the diversity of the Syracuse University community, and become integrated into this community.

Social and Academic Integration. The Office of Residence Services for years has provided programming that focuses on student development. Areas of student development include autonomy, personal responsibility, relationships, self-concept, intellect, and purpose (Baker and others, 1987). The theme of diversity will be integrated into the residence life orientation within the context of these developmental areas. A similar priority has been set regarding the identification of academic life developmental areas and the identification of ways to help academic faculty and staff keep them in mind when interacting with students.

Quality of Instruction. At a more general level, another academic life priority is to improve the quality of undergraduate instruction. The Teaching Assistant Orientation Program mentioned earlier is one attempt to accomplish this. The establishment of the Gateway Program, which provides funds and other support for the improvement of lower-division courses, is also related to this priority. A grant recently received from the Sears Roebuck Foundation provides funds for the development of a program to prepare academic unit heads (such as departmental chairs) to play a proactive role in the improvement of undergraduate instruction. There are also numerous course, curriculum, and program developmental projects supported by the Center for Instructional Development that have a direct positive impact on undergraduate education and, it is hoped, on student retention as well.

Student Support. Programs to support special populations were also identified as priorities. The Syracuse University Office of Student Support and Development operates programs for a wide variety of students including academically and financially disadvantaged minority students. Recently programs have been funded to provide support for regularly admitted minority students in science and professional areas and for minority students who wish to pursue graduate education. These programs provide various types of academic, financial, and personal support for students who in the past were not eligible for such support.

Impact. Because many of these institutional programs are new, information on their impact is only beginning to be collected. The following subsections briefly describe impact studies relative to these planning efforts.

Admissions. Working with the Syracuse City School District, data on those students in the Syracuse Challenge and appropriate comparison groups are being analyzed to determine if the program increases high school grade point averages, high school retention, participation in college preparatory programs, and other student outcomes.

Orientation and Other Integration Issues. The impact of the first offering of the freshmen orientation program was assessed in the fall of 1988. Additional data will be collected during the spring of 1989. And a thorough evaluation will be conducted of the fall 1989 program. In addition, a comprehensive longitudinal study of freshmen is being constructed. It is guided by a dynamic model that includes: (1) the skills, knowledge, and attitudes that students bring to their college experience; (2) their developmental progress and the experiences they have at Syracuse University; and (3) the outcomes of the interaction of these variables. Data regarding the variables will be collected several times during their freshman year, periodically during the rest of their time at Syracuse University, and after they leave Syracuse University as graduates, stop-outs, or dropouts. This study is being designed to draw together information collected in many different ways about students before, during, and after their Syracuse University involvement.

Quality of Instruction. The Sears Roebuck Project's impact on the quality of undergraduate instruction will be measured in two ways. One is through the campuswide surveying of faculty perceptions regarding the importance of undergraduate teaching both before and after the project. In addition, profiles based on a set of indicators of teaching importance will be developed for those departments chosen to participate in the project. These profiles will be used to indicate areas of strength and weakness, to direct improvement efforts, and to document whether or not improvements have in fact occurred.

Student Support. Comprehensive program evaluations, which include the assessment of impact, are also being conducted for the special-population programs. For example, a formative evaluation of the program for students in the sciences and professional programs is being pursued. In addition, a study of the persistence, graduation rates, and grade point averages of these students in comparison with other comparable students is under way.

A variety of new projects are undertaken each year as more Syracuse University central administrators learn how valuable the types of data collected can be.

Conclusion

It is important not to get caught up in the debate over the definition and role of assessment itself but instead to focus on the use of a systematic process of data collection to provide the information needed to address a variety of concerns in higher education. The development of existing and new courses, curricula, and programs, as well as the resolution of administrative concerns and institutional issues, can be served by a wealth of systematically collected information in addition to data on student outcomes.

As discussed extensively in each chapter of this sourcebook, many lessons that have been learned over the years in evaluation and other fields can be applied to the issues raised by the current assessment movement. The research and evaluation office of the Center for Instructional Development is but one example of a campus unit that has used a systematic data collection process to provide quality information relevant to concerns in higher education. The appropriate current and future role of those in assessment should be to broaden its purpose and diversify its processes by taking advantage of the many lessons learned in other fields and in agencies like the center.

References

Baker, B., Conlon, J., Cummings, J., Decker, S., Deters, K., and Shrimplin, J. *A Study of First-Year College Students Attending Syracuse University.* Syracuse, N.Y.: Office of Residence Services, Syracuse University, 1987.

Centra, J., Froh, R. C., Gray, P. J., and Lambert, L. M. *Evaluating Teaching for Promotion and Tenure.* Littleton, Mass.: Copley, 1987.

Diamond, R. M. *Designing and Improving Courses and Curricula in Higher Education: A Systematic Approach.* San Francisco: Jossey-Bass, 1989.

Diamond, R. M., and Gray, P. J. "A National Study of Teaching Assistants." Paper presented at the annual meeting of the Association for the Study of Higher Education, Baltimore, November 23, 1987. (ED 292 360; HE 020 284)

Ewell, P. T. "Assessment: Where Are We?" *Change*, January/February 1987, pp. 23-28.

Marchese, T. J. "An Update on Assessment." *AAHE Bulletin*, December 1983, pp. 3-8.

Molotsky, I. F. "Assessing Assessment: The Faculty Perspective." *AAUP*, 1988, 7 (2), 4-5.

Rogler, D. K., and Gray, P. J. "The Syracuse University Teaching Assistant Orientation Program: An Evaluation Report." Syracuse, N.Y.: Center for Instructional Development, Syracuse University, 1989.

Southern Association of Colleges and Schools. *Criteria for Accreditation.* (5th ed.) Decatur, Ga.: Southern Association of Colleges and Schools, 1988.

Peter J. Gray is director of evaluation and research at the Syracuse University Center for Instructional Development, and he is a member of the American Evaluation Association board of directors.

Robert M. Diamond is assistant vice-chancellor for instructional development and director of the Center for Instructional Development at Syracuse University.

While some guidelines and caveats can be garnered from the theory and practice of others, each institution is faced with resolving some key issues that will help shape the future of assessment in higher education.

Making Assessment Work: A Synthesis and Future Directions

G. Roger Sell

The other chapters in this sourcebook discuss a wide range of practices and issues dealing with assessment in higher education institutions. Not all of the authors share a similar perspective, or even definition, of assessment. To some extent, each author provides a unique view of assessment and what makes it work. This concluding chapter attempts to synthesize a few recommendations by authors in this volume and to highlight key issues for the future of assessment in colleges and universities.

A Synthesis of Recommended Practices

Among the authors of this volume, there appears to be consensus or near consensus on at least seven guidelines and caveats for effective assessment practices.

1. *While assessment may be a response to external demands and audiences, its locus and main effects are within the institution.* Whether stimulated by state-mandated programs, accreditation or program review, or other sources external to the institution, the examples of assessment activities provided in the previous chapters represent assessment as an institu-

tional function. The authors are cautious, however, in discussing the purposes that assessment serves and point out that one assessment purpose may displace or distort another. Institutions should be reflective about competing motives for assessment and attempt to weigh not only what is demanded of them by external audiences but also what is in the best interests of the institution and its members. Furthermore, assessment activities require valuable resources in the form of personnel as well as financial resources used for equipment, space, and information. While assessment activities can and do have effects beyond the institutions, their immediate main effects, including costs and benefits, are within the institution.

2. *Assessment can be designed to serve multiple purposes, but its ultimate purpose is improvement.* Chapter One identifies several purposes that assessment can serve and suggests a major distinction between intentions that are formative (improvement or developmental in nature) and those that are summative (designed primarily for accountability, resource allocation, certification, personnel decision, and so forth). Examples of assessment activities undertaken at the universities of Illinois, Syracuse, and Western Michigan illustrate multiple purposes that assessment attempts to serve at those institutions. The main thrust of arguments and rationale provided through these examples, as well as the discussions by Braskamp and Sell, is that the use of assessment to improve and develop performance (of students, faculty, departments or programs, and institutions) lies at the heart of vitality in colleges and universities. If we paraphrase Cronbach's (1963) advice with a slight adaptation, I think most of the other authors would agree with this statement: The greatest service assessment can perform is to identify aspects of performance where improvement is desirable; assessment, used to improve performance in a timely and appropriate manner, contributes more to the quality of education than assessment after the fact.

3. *Properly conducted assessment practices emphasize utilization of information.* Assessment information that is not used is wasted. Several of the authors in this volume have offered explicit suggestions for enhancing the utilization of assessment information. Some of these suggestions include the following:
- Attend to institutional characteristics and readiness to change in the design and implementation of assessment strategies.
- Take steps to ensure that assessment data are valid, reliable, and credible.
- Provide information that is understandable, concise, and timely.
- Involve potential audiences (users) in the process from the beginning, provide opportunities for ongoing discussion of findings, and identify one or more concerned individuals who will provide leadership to ensure that the findings are acted on.

- Provide feedback and consultation (if possible) that include suggestions and alternatives for change and anticipate and accommodate differences among the users of assessment information.

4. *Participation by stakeholders is essential to successful assessment practices.* Stakeholders are those who have significant responsibility for or are in other ways relatively directly affected by an assessment. The authors of this volume advocate participatory assessment, where stakeholders play a central role both in designing the assessment and in interpreting, discussing, and using the results. There are some differences of opinion among the authors whether those conducting assessment should be treated as stakeholders in the process, a point discussed later in this chapter. As Braskamp describes it, the involvement of stakeholders creates a sense of ownership and, with it, some feeling of control or influence over their destiny. I have pointed out in Chapter Two that assessments may not get off the ground, much less be used and useful, without some coalition building and cooperation among those affected by assessment practices and findings.

5. *Effective assessment practices are usually accompanied by an arsenal of diverse and flexible assessment strategies, adapted to a particular institution and application.* Ory and Braskamp are perhaps strongest in emphasizing the need for multiple and diverse assessment strategies. In addition, examples from the three institutions highlighted in Chapters Four, Five, and Six demonstrate that assessment approaches are indeed diverse in practice. These examples illustrate a considerable variety of data, methods, sources, and criteria used in serving multiple purposes and audiences within an institution. As Braskamp clearly states, there is no single best method or model to assess performance, whether it be the performance of faculty, students, programs, or the institution itself. I would follow this by arguing that a given assessment approach should be adapted to or developed for a particular use and context; assessment methodology (instruments, procedures, and so forth) should not dictate or lead an assessment but rather should follow from its particular purpose, audience, sources of data, and institutional context. Furthermore, it is often useful to corroborate and extend assessment information with more than one method. Since there is a wide range of assessment questions that might guide an inquiry (see Chapter One for question examples), it seems clear that an arsenal of assessment strategies should be available or under development for an institution or program of some sophistication.

6. *The costs of assessment should be weighed against its potential benefits and side effects.* While my previous chapter in this volume is the only one that directly addresses the issue of assessment costs compared to benefits or consequences, several authors touch on this important aspect of assessment. For example, Braskamp suggests (through reference to Robert Stake) that administrators should shoulder the burden of demonstrating

that the positive effects of assessment outweigh the costs. I have argued in Chapter Two that often too little attention is given to the issue of balance among competing needs for assessment and faculty and administrator responsibilities for teaching, research, public service, and other activities they perform. Somehow, the benefits of assessment must be related to a complex milieu within institutions where cause-and-effect models may be inadequate or inappropriate to use.

There are several aspects of costs that might be considered. These include financial costs (fixed/variable, marginal/total, opportunity, and so forth), social costs (such as high levels of stress in interpersonal relations that have a negative effect on a healthy institutional environment), and psychological costs (such as diminutions of self-worth resulting from negative feedback or from decisions made without adequate explanations and/or assistance for improvement). Few institutions have reliable data even about the financial costs of their current assessment practices, let alone their social and psychological costs.

Assessment can have many benefits (anticipated and unanticipated), individually and collectively. On the down side, assessment can also have unintended side effects, such as unhealthy competition among individuals and organizational units, practices that are perceived as encroaching on privacy or academic freedom, and dissipation of energy through activities that are viewed as duplicative, redundant, or unnecessary. Many of ill effects of assessment can be eliminated or reduced through the practices recommended by the authors in this sourcebook. However, a sound institutional approach to assessment will also give systematic attention and reflection to both the costs and outcomes of assessment activities.

7. *Those who practice assessment can benefit from a knowledge of evaluation theory and methodology.* A central thesis of Chapter One is that those who undertake assessments in higher education can benefit from what has been learned in the field (some might say the discipline) of evaluation. My sense is that Davis views most of what is called student outcomes assessment as representing the measurement or testing school of evaluation, which she believes is not the mainstream of evaluation as practiced today. Most of the other chapter authors readily mix the terms assessment and evaluation, although Dennison and Bunda are more cautious in this respect, and Ory describes assessment as a component of a larger evaluation program. While an intense preoccupation with the possible semantic differences between assessment and evaluation is not productive in my view, there may be subtle underlying issues and values that can be very significant in practice (a point I will return to shortly). For now, my advice is to reduce the "noise" by sidestepping petty differences or idiosyncratic preferences and to get on with the business of making assessment work. In doing so, I believe that the boundary lines will begin to disappear between those who insist that assessment and

evaluation are really different in nature, that advocates of assessment and evaluation will have much in common, and that both can learn from one another. In this respect, the theory and methodology of evaluation have much to offer those in the assessment enterprise.

Future Directions for Assessment

I do not have a crystal ball for predicting the future, and, if I did, it no doubt would be cloudy. Other authors in this volume and many others who have not written here are equally qualified to comment on assumptions and forecasts about the future of assessment in higher education institutions. While I draw on comments in the preceding chapters, what I have to say is primarily my own version of the future of assessment and the key issues that will help shape it.

A Macroperspective on Assessment. There are two hypotheses (or testable assumptions) that guide my thinking about the future of assessment in colleges and universities: The external conditions and demands for assessment are not likely to decrease in the foreseeable future; and, to make best use of scarce resources (particularly human resources) amid competing values and purposes, institutions will struggle to make assessment work.

Whether from the viewpoint of a student, a taxpayer, a legislator, an employer, a state or federal agency, an alumnus, a trustee, or a donor, the cost and quality of higher education is of great national and international concern. The perceived interrelatedness of higher education and other segments of society and the expectations for higher education institutions are not likely to decrease over the next few years. I think it is a safe bet that assessment, its kin, and its future relatives will be on the agenda of external stakeholders of higher education institutions for years to come.

There is also considerable evidence that institutions are taking assessment, not limited to student outcomes assessment, seriously. Great expenditures of time and effort (sometimes to outwit institutional critics and assessment advocates) are already being given to assessment in its many forms. Yet it is not at all clear, with a few unusual exceptions like Alverno College, that assessment as currently practiced contributes much to the enhancement of institutional and individual effectiveness. Cohesiveness and useful institutional strategies for assessment that are subscribed to by a large portion of each college and university community are hard to come by.

Still, I believe that most administrators and faculty are beginning to accept the reality that some degree of assessment is necessary in institutional life. What it will now be more difficult for institutions to achieve is a careful balance of (1) activities such as teaching, research, and public service; (2) assessment for summative purposes (accountability, resource allocation, personnel decisions, and so forth); and (3) assessment for formative purposes (improvement and development of individual, programs, and institutions). Most institutions are entering a long-term struggle to balance the demands for assessment with other institutional responsibilities and to obtain some reasonable degree of compatibility (if not synergy) between formative and summative assessments.

An Intrainstitutional Perspective on Assessment. Beyond these general, macro-level observations, I would like to identify six issues that in my estimation will shape the future of assessment as we know it today. What I am suggesting is that each institution must continue to wrestle with these issues and resolve them to some extent if it wishes to become proficient at useful assessment practices. These issues, each with a current and future (or imperative) perspective, include:

- What is (will be, should be) the status of assessment at my institution?
- How does (will, should) assessment support my institution's multiple programs, audiences, purposes, and members?
- Under what conditions are (will, should) assessments (be) affordable compared to their outcomes and effects for my institution?
- How does (will, should) my institution develop or improve its assessment capabilities over time, with attention to both summative and formative purposes?
- Which means of organizing and conducting assessment does (will, should) my institution use?
- Who does (will, should) provide leadership and support for the practice of assessment at my institution?

To some extent, other chapters in this sourcebook have addressed, albeit incompletely, aspects of five of these six issues. The remainder of this chapter begins to provide some additional thoughts on perhaps the most pervasive of these issues and the one that is the most reasonable starting point for most institutions: What is (will be, should be) the status of assessment at my institution?

Throughout the literature on assessment over the past decade or more, the dominant focus has been on student outcomes and the use of measurement instruments and procedures (highly quantitative in emphasis) of one kind or another as the primary methodology. This volume extends the discussion of assessment beyond student outcomes and includes a broad range of expanded subjects—institutional environments, processes, and programs, as well as faculty and staff. In addition, several of the authors have argued for a much greater emphasis on qualitative data and methods to address and more adequately respond to certain kinds of assessment questions. It is reasonable to expect that administrators and faculty on the front lines become confused, if not frustrated and disenchanted, with the seemingly endless barrage of fragmented information about what assessment is, what others think institutions should be doing, and who should be doing what. Each institution is faced with making sense of what assessment means, what its current status is, and what it will and should become.

I think that it is necessary to break down the broader question about the status of assessment at any one institution into several more manageable questions, two of which are: What is (will be, should be) the primary focus of assessment at my institution? And which key roles does (will, should) assessment perform at my institution? There are other important questions that could be raised about the status of assessment for a particular institution, but many of these questions are embedded within the other five issues already identified. I will draw on the previous chapters to illustrate options that an institution may wish to consider in responding to the two subquestions related to the status of assessment.

Regarding the primary focus for assessment, institutions may wish to concentrate attention primarily on student outcomes or a broader array of institutional environments, processes, programs, and personnel that include but go beyond students and related information about them. Regarding the key roles for assessment, institutions may wish to stress description and analysis, the judgment of merit or worth, and/or negotiation among stakeholders; Lincoln (1988) provides a short history of the evolution of these roles.

Based on explicit definitions and examples provided in the preceding chapters, I see that Davis, Dennison, and Bunda (Chapters One and Four) use the term *assessment* to focus more on student outcomes and related information, while the other authors focus more on other institutional concerns. There certainly is an overlap in the references to assessment and examples provided by the different authors. While one author may focus on student outcomes, it is likely that the same author will also describe information that is needed about the institution, its faculty, and its programs. Similarly, those authors who tend to begin with an institutional perspective on assessment frequently return to student outcomes and other student characteristics when they describe faculty, program, or institutional assessment.

So where does an institution wish to focus its assessment? Figure 1 shows examples of various assessment topics that have been identified by authors of this sourcebook. Given such a lengthy list of potential topics (and others not on the list), each institution must be rather selective in where to focus its attention. One starting place is to identify assessment activities that are under way or are being considered at the institution. Another starting place is to identify actions that are or will be considered by the institution and that are related to one or more facets of assessment. A third approach is to examine an institution's relative balance of assessment activities within the four large groupings (student, faculty, program, institution).

Figure 1. Examples of Assessment Topics Found in This Sourcebook

Topic	Davis	Sell	Braskamp	Gray/ Diamond	Ory	Dennison/ Bunda
Student-Related Assessment						
Entering characteristics	X	X				
Placement/proficiency	X	X			X	X
Gender education outcomes		X				X
Performance by majors						X
Alumni satisfaction						X
Attrition/retention	X	X		X		
Campus life		X		X		
Learning activities			X			
Faculty-Related Assessment						
Teaching		X		X		
Performance/outcomes		X		X		
Instructors					X	
Activities/effort		X	X			
Responsibilities		X				
Workloads		X				
Promotion and tenure		X				
Salary increases		X				
Awards		X				
Development		X				
Program-Related Assessment						
Academic programs	X	X			X	X
Academic support programs		X				
Courses/curricula	X	X	X	X	X	
Student services programs	X			X		
Student services facilities				X		
Transition program					X	
Honors program					X	
International teaching assistant (ITA) program					X	
Institution-Related Assessment						
Campus environment		X				X
Campus culture		X	X			
Financial resources		X	X			
Human resources		X				
Physical resources		X				
Information resources		X				
External environment		X				
Administrator performance					X	

The question about assessment roles is even more complex and problematic than that about assessment focus. This is partly because assessment (or evaluation) is sometimes thought of as a process or activity without reference to who performs it, sometimes as a distinct study or problem, and sometimes as a domain of responsibility (or expertise) belonging to a person, position, committee, office, or program.

The evaluation literature, some of which is cited throughout the chapters, is strewn with a long and weaving line of discussion and controversy about "the proper role of evaluators." While I will not go into the several facets of these rather heated debates over the years, including many significant concerns about the ethics and credibility of evaluators, I want to endorse the importance of each assessment role and to suggest that institutions should try to ensure that each role is present somewhere in the assessment process. I would summarize this by saying that more than one individual, group, or office at each institution needs to collect, store, retrieve, describe, analyze, and report assessment data; to make judgments about the merit and/or worth of that which is being assessed; and to negotiate among stakeholders for the purposes and questions that will guide assessments, determining how assessments will be designed and conducted, what will be reported (and to whom, how, and when), and what the costs and outcomes will be.

Several offices in your college or university may be involved with assessment in one capacity or another. Figure 2 provides examples of types of offices that are known to be assessment data collectors and users across institutions. They include offices in areas such as academic affairs, business and administration, computing, fund raising, instructional support, personnel services, and student services. As the status of assessment is examined at your institution, you may wish to use such a checklist to locate the variety of data bases and potential participants for assessment.

In concluding this chapter, I would like to return to an issue hinted at throughout this discussion: Who are the practitioners of assessment in higher education? Although I have not done a systematic review of authors in the literature or speeches on assessment, my bet is that those who most frequently write and speak about assessment are specialists in testing and consulting firms, federally sponsored programs, state agencies, and universities. I doubt whether national leadership of assessment is being exercised by representatives of the rank-and-file faculty or the administration in colleges and universities. Yet, if my earlier hypotheses are confirmed, the future of assessment will depend on the combined successes and failures of individual institutions and the practices that are developed, adopted, and used by faculty and administrators.

I am not saying that we should do away with assessment (evaluation) specialists or offices that provide these services. But, if assessment is to serve its ultimate purpose—improvement and development of individuals

Figure 2. Examples of Institutional Offices That Could Serve as Assessment Data Collectors or Users

Office Area	Examples of Offices
Academic affairs	College Department Division, school, or center Graduate studies Professional studies Provost Undergraduate studies
Business and administration	Campus planning and space utilization Controller Course and classroom scheduling Financial planning Institutional planning Institutional research Purchasing
Computing	Administrative computing Instructional computing Research computing
Fund raising	Alumni relations Corporate relations Development fund Sponsored research
Instructional support services	Developmental education Evaluation and testing Faculty development Instructional development Library Learning resources
Personnel services	Affirmative action Benefits Minority affairs Staff development
Student services	Counseling Financial aid Health Placement Recruitment Registration Student life

and organizations—then the primary actors for both conducting assessments and using the results from them should be folks in the trenches. I am for admitting assessment specialists into the act as full partners, who are committed to the mission and goals of their institution and wish to use their special skills to develop and enhance it. However, I predict that the biggest gains will be made when a significant number of faculty and administrators at each institution also consider themselves to be knowledgeable practitioners of assessment and do not rely on specialists to make assessment work.

References

Cronbach, L. J. "Course Improvement Through Evaluation." *Teachers College Record*, 1963, *64*, 672-683.

Lincoln, Y. S. "Can Somebody Give Me a Hand Here? Program Review, Accreditation Process, and Outcome Assessment as the Straws That Are Breaking the Camel's Back." Paper presented at the annual meeting of the Association for the Study of Higher Education, St. Louis, Mo., November 3, 1988.

G. Roger Sell is senior program director for organizational development in the Center for Teaching Excellence at The Ohio State University.

Index

A

Abedor, A. J., 36, 38
Academic Profile, by ETS, 86
Accreditation, 27
Achievement Tests, by ETS, 79, 80
Adelman, C., 7, 18, 21, 38, 52, 69
Administrators: and assessment, 54-55, 65; concerns, 97-102; effectiveness, 76; evaluation system, 76-77; turnover, 77
Advanced Placement Program (APP) of the College Board, 80
Alkin, M. C., 18
Alverno College, 53, 54, 66
American Testing Service (ATS), 60
Applebaum, M. I., 17, 19
Arns, R. G., 23, 27, 38
Assessment: and accountability, 53, 54; affordable, 34-35; and change, 32-36, 55; conducting, 16-17; consequences of, 45-46; cost-benefits, 30-31; criteria, 14-15; critique of, 24-28; data, 63, 73; defined, 7, 22, 51; effective, 33-37, 66-69; and evaluation, 6-18; and excellence, 47-48; faculty, 23, 25-26, 45-46; focus of, 44-45; future, 113-119; goals of, 9-11, 48, 55-56; guidelines for program, 44-47; and higher education, 22, 89-107; incentives/disincentives, 32-33; institutional, 23, 27-28, 44, 49, 52, 54-56; intrainstitutional perspective, 114-119; macro perspective, 113-114; meaning of, 7-8, 22-23; methods, 17-18; model, 28-29; organizational perspective of, 21-38; and organizational realities, 29-33; participatory, 46-47; practices, 109-113; program, 23, 26-27, 72-85, 92-97; purpose of, 8-9, 54; questions, 11-14; recent developments in, 5; socio-political pressures for, 6, 10, 32, 35; stakeholders, 15-16; standards, 18; student, 7, 23, 24-25; support, 31-32, 37; talent-development, 14-15; terminology, 8; at U.C. Berkeley, 10; value-added, 14-15; at Western Michigan University, 56-59. *See also* Evaluation; Program evaluation
Astin, A. W., 7, 8, 19, 37, 39
Ayala, F., 7, 8, 19

B

Baird, L. L., 11, 15, 19
Baker, B., 105, 107
Baldridge, J. V., 21, 39
Banta, T. W., 5, 16, 19
Barak, R. J., 23, 39
Becker, H. S., 24, 39
Beidler, P. G., 23, 39
Belcher, M. J., 5, 7, 16, 19
Bennett, J. G., 23, 26, 39
Bess, J. L., 34, 39
Blau, P. M., 21, 39
Blumenstyk, G., 5, 29
Bok, D. C., 1, 3, 53, 69
Boyer, C. M., 7, 8, 9, 19
Brandenburg, D. C., 49, 50, 72, 87
Braskamp, L. A., 18, 19, 44, 49, 50, 72, 87
Bray, D., 5, 7, 16, 19
Brown, R. D., 18, 19

C

Cameron, K. S., 34, 39
Carey, R. G., 8, 20
Centra, J. A., 23, 39, 100, 107
Chandler, J. W., 7, 19
Chater, S. S., 23, 39
Clark, B. R., 33, 36, 39
Clayton State College, 54
Cohen, M. D., 21, 39
College Board, 79-80
Colleges: assessment efforts, 75; effectiveness evaluations, 10; evaluation programs, 74-87; honors program, 81-82; pressure on, 7; and student placement, 79-80; teaching-oriented, 46. *See also* Institutions

121

Collegiate Assessment of Academic Proficiency, by ACT, 63-64
COMP test, by ACT, 86
Conlon, J., 107
Conrad, C. F., 23, 26, 31, 39
Course: development, 92-96; evaluation, 77-79; redesign, 94-96
Cronbach, L. J., 110, 119
Cross, K. P., 45, 50

D

Daillak, R., 18
Davey, K. B., 25, 39
Davis, B. G., 17, 19
Decker, S., 107
Deters, K., 107
Deters, S., 107
Diamond, R. M., 91, 93, 95, 96, 107

E

Eison, J. A., 7, 19, 24, 40
El-Khawas, E., 6, 20
English as a Second Language (ESL), 84
Evaluation: and assessment, 6-18, 51; college effectiveness, 10; defined, 7; formative/summative, 8-9, 24; program, 44-47, 52, 55, 72-87; and stakeholders, 11. *See also* Assessment; Program evaluation
Ewell, P. T., 1, 3, 5, 6, 7, 8, 9, 14, 16, 17, 19, 21, 31, 37, 39, 52, 69, 70, 89, 107

F

Faculty: assessment, 23, 25-26, 45-46; -based evaluation, 74-76; improvement, 47; ratings by students, 77-79; and staff differences, 46; and student learning, 45; use of assessment results, 55. *See also* Teaching
Fincher, C., 34, 39
Forrest, A., 60, 70
Freeman, H. E., 8, 20
French, R. P., 33, 39
Froh, R. C., 100, 107
Fund for the Improvement of Postsecondary Education (FIPSE), 5

G

Geer, B., 24, 39
George Mason University, 54
Graduate Record Examination (GRE), 12, 52
Gray, P. J., 96, 97, 100, 107
Green, K.C.A., 23, 40
Guba, E. G., 15, 17, 19, 20

H

Hackman, J. R., 44, 50
Halpern, D. F., 5, 15, 16, 19, 30, 40, 54, 70
Hanson, G. R., 15, 19
Hartle, T. W., 22, 40
Higher education: assessment, 10, 22-23, 32, 38; decision making, 71-87; failings of, 6; future of, 38; improving, 89-107; policy making, 85-86; quality, 37; strains in, 32. *See also* Colleges; Institutions; Student
Hughes, E. C., 24, 39
Hutchings, P., 1, 4, 17, 19

I

Institutions: and assessment, 23, 27-28, 44, 49, 52, 54-56; costs, 31; culture, 47-48; data bases, 27-28; effectiveness, 44, 49; and excellence, 47; ideal of self-assessing, 28-29; issues, 103-106; and personal investment theory, 44; politics, 32, 35; realities of, 29-33. *See also* Colleges

J

Jacobi, M., 7, 8, 19
Joint Committee on Standards for Educational Evaluation, 7, 18, 19
Jones, D. P., 31, 37, 39

K

Karren, R. J., 45, 50
Krug, S., 44, 50

L

Lambert, L. M., 100, 107
Law School Admission Test (LSAT), 12
Lawler, E. E., III, 44, 50
Lawrence, B., 37, 40
Lawrence, J. K., 23, 40
Leadership: activities, 44; and assessment, 33-34. *See also* Administrators
Learning: -oriented institutions, 54; outcomes, 86-87; and student assessment, 24. *See also* Teaching
Licata, C. M., 23, 40
Lincoln, Y. S., 15, 17, 19, 20, 115, 119
Loacker, G., 24, 25, 40, 53, 70

M

McCartt, A. T., 40
McMillan, J. H., 15, 20, 23, 40
Maehr, L. M., 44, 50
Mandelbaum, S. J., 34, 40
March, J. G., 21, 39
Marchese, T. J., 1, 4, 7, 20, 92, 107
Measurement, 51-52
Medical College Admission Test (MCAT), 12
Mentkowski, M., 17, 20, 53, 70
Mento, A. J., 45, 50
Micek, S. S., 23, 40
Miller, R. I., 17, 20, 25, 40
Millett, S. D., 21, 40
Milton, O., 24, 40

N

National Assessment of Educational Progress, 8
National Center for Education Statistics, 38
National Center for Higher Education Management Systems (NCHEMS), 37
National Governors' Association, 5, 6, 7, 20
National Institute of Education, 1, 4
Nevo, D., 6, 14, 15, 16, 20
North Central Association of Colleges and Schools, 27, 40
Northeast Missouri State University, 54

O

Ohio Board of Regents, 23, 40
Ory, J. C., 49, 50, 72, 87
Outcomes Measurement Program (ACT-COMP), by ACT, 60, 63, 64

P

Palladino, J., 7, 19
Parker, S. A., 86, 87
Pascarella, E. T., 15, 20
Patterson, V. W., 37, 40
Patton, M. Q., 17, 18, 20
Pfeffer, J., 31, 40
Poland, W., 23, 27, 38
Pollio, H. R., 24, 40
Popham, W. J., 72, 87
Program evaluation: credibility, 72; development, 72-74, 92-97; examples, 44-47, 52, 55; flexibility, 73-74; and organizational fit, 72; outcomes, 76; transition, 80-81; at UIUC, 72-85; utility, 72-73
Putnam, J. F., 38, 40

R

Raven, B., 33, 39
Rogler, I. F., 97, 107
Rohrbaugh, J., 40
Rossi, P. H., 8, 20
Rossman, J. E., 6, 20

S

Sachs, S. G., 36, 38
Salancik, G. R., 31, 40
Schön, D. A., 47, 50
Scriven, M., 8, 20, 25, 41
Sell, G. R., 25, 38, 39, 40
Shalock, H. D., 40
Shirley, R. C., 23, 41
Shrimplin, J., 107
Smith, N. L., 17, 20
Southern Association of Colleges and Schools, 103, 107
Spangehl, S. D., 1, 4

SPEAK test, by ETS, 82-84
Stakeholders, 11, 15
Standard of Written English test, by ETS, 80
Stanford Diagnostic Reading Test, by Psychological Corporation, 80
Steele, J., 60, 70
Steele, R. P., 45, 50
Student: advisement, 14; assessment, 7, 23, 24-25; attrition, 12-13, 104; grades, 24; international, orientation, 82-84; learning, 11-12; outcomes, 22, 27, 49; placement, 79-80; ratings of instructors, 77-79; university, enrollment, 11; values, 12
Student Group on the Conditions of Excellence in American Higher Education, 24, 41
Stufflebeam, D. L., 6, 20
Syracuse University Center for Instructional Development, 91, 95-98, 102, 105-106

T

Teaching: assistants, 82-84, 96-97, 102; effective, 78; evaluating, 49; guiding principle of, 45; improving, 78-79; quality, 13, 78; and student assessment, 25. *See also* Faculty
Test of College Preparatory Mathematics, by Illinois Universities, 84

Test of Spoken English (TSE), by ETS, 82
Tucker, A., 26, 41
Tuckman, H. P., 25, 41

U

Universities. *See* Colleges
University of California, Berkeley, 10-11
University of Illinois, Urbana-Champaign (UIUC), 71, 78-87
University of Tennessee at Knoxville, 54

V

Volkwein, J. F., 23, 41

W

Warren, J., 15, 20
Weathersby, G., 37, 40
Western Michigan University (WMU), 56-69
Westling, J., 6, 20
White, P., 18
Wildavsky, A., 28, 29, 32, 33, 34-35, 37, 41, 47, 50
Wilson, R. F., 23, 26, 31, 39
Workplace: changes, 6; and employee productivity, 44

3382